nobu
WEST

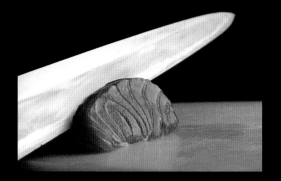

First published in 2006 by Quadrille Publishing Limited, Alhambra
House, 27-31 Charing Cross Road, London WC2H 0LS

Text © 2006 by Matsuhisa Nobu and Mark Edwards
Photography © 2006 by Eiichi Takahashi
Edited text, design, and layout © 2006 by Quadrille Publishing Ltd

07 08 09 10 11 TWP 10 9 8 7 6 5 4 3 2 1

ISBN-13: 978-0-7407-6547-6
ISBN-10: 0-7407-6547-7

Library of Congress Control Number: 2006047827

www.andrewsmcmeel.com

Editorial director	Jane O'Shea
Creative director	Helen Lewis
Editor and project manager	Lewis Esson
Art direction and design	Vanessa Courtier
Photography	Eiichi Takahashi
Food styling	Nobu Matsuhisa and Mark Edwards
Production	Ruth Deary

nobu
WEST

Nobu Matsuhisa
Mark Edwards

photographs by Eiichi Takahashi

**Andrews McMeel
Publishing, LLC**
Kansas City

contents

Contents

cocktails

sauces

glossary, index

Introduction

These days, cooking styles are not limited to their location and/or ingredients. With the Nobu restaurants now totaling sixteen worldwide, each new restaurant explores a fresh range of local ingredients and, in turn, contributes new ideas to the others. It's like a recipe book that is always growing.

Nobu West, the third book in the series, explores even more fully the confluence of cultures and cuisines that is now "Nobu-style" cuisine. Although the recipes in it are still quintessentially Japanese in style and technique, the ingredients are much more those found mostly in the West.

The recipes are a result of not only our exploration of ingredients found in Europe and the Americas, but of our application of various creative approaches borne of knowledge gained from the distinct cuisines in the different countries in which we operate, to make Nobu-style cuisine more accessible to a wider audience.

As well as drawing on more readily available ingredients, we have attempted greater simplicity in the approach to the recipes to make it easier for you, the reader, to re-create and capture these dishes in the same fresh and vibrant manner as they were created. We hope you enjoy—even have fun—discovering and cooking the Nobu-style dishes that follow.

We would like to thank all our suppliers who contributed the ingredients for this book, as well as the staff at Nobu London and Nobu Berkeley Street, without whose efforts this book would not have been possible. Also, a big "thank you" to photographer Eiichi Takahashi for his amazing talent of capturing the moment and the essence of Nobu cuisine.

Nobuyuki Matsuhisa
Mark Edwards

London, July 2006

cold appetizers

Abalone and White Peach Shooters

This chilled soup is served as a "shooter" in a tall sherry glass, like our very popular oyster and quail egg shooters. Abalone meat can be very tough when raw, but this soup actually has a very silky texture, as both the abalone and the mountain yam are finely grated.

The Japanese mountain yam, or *yama imo*, is also known as "sticky yam," and this property does help bind the liquid and give the soup a bit of body. For the flavor, it is important that you use white peach.

serves 4

stock

1³/4 cups Dashi (see page 17)

1/4 teaspoon sea salt

2 tablespoons sake

2 tablespoons light soy sauce

1/8 cucumber, diced

4 cherry tomatoes, diced

1 white peach, peeled, pitted, and diced

2 fresh abalone, shelled and cleaned

1¹/2-inch piece of mountain yam (yama-imo, see page 253)

1   Make the stock by mixing all the ingredients together and chill.

2   When ready to serve, spoon into 4 chilled small sherry glasses equal amounts of the diced cucumber, tomatoes, and white peach.

3   Grate the abalone into a bowl using the fine mesh of a cheese grater. (It can also be chopped by hand, but it must be very fine.)

4   Grate the yam into the bowl using the fine cheese grater again; this will cause it to become very slimy.

5   Mix enough of the stock with the grated abalone and the yam to create a loose soup and then pour into the glasses to serve.

Chilled Pea Shoot Soup with Caviar

This soup makes a very refreshing way to start a meal, encapsulating the wonderful flavor of pea shoots when in season with a Japanese-flavored soup base. The addition of caviar turns the soup into something quite special, and it should be served very cold and in small portions.

serves 4

soup base (Dashi)
1/6 ounce (5g) konbu (dried seaweed, see page 251)
2 cups water
1/2 ounce dried bonito flakes (see page 250)

5 ounces pea shoots (see note, right; try to select the smallest shoots)
crushed ice, to serve
2 teaspoons light soy sauce
sea salt and freshly ground black pepper
3/4 ounce Golden Oscietra caviar

1 First make the soup base. Wipe the konbu with a damp cloth to remove any salt residue. In a nonreactive saucepan, heat 2 cups water and the konbu slowly over medium heat.

2 Just before the water comes to a boil, take out the konbu and add the bonito flakes, then turn off the heat and let stand for 20 to 30 minutes.

3 Strain through a cheesecloth-lined strainer.

4 In the rinsed-out pan, bring the dashi to a simmer, remove from the heat, and add the pea shoots; let stand for 5 minutes. Pour the pan contents into a blender and blend at high speed until smooth. (Be very careful to hold the lid down with a kitchen cloth, as this mixture is hot, or wait until the soup is cold before blending.) Strain the soup through a fine strainer and refrigerate until very cold.

5 To serve, place 4 soup cups in a bowl of crushed ice to chill. Stir the soy sauce and salt and pepper to taste into the chilled soup, then pour the soup into the chilled cups, leaving room for the caviar. Spoon the caviar equally on top of the soup.

note Pea shoots, the young tender leaves and tendrils at the tips of the pea plant, have been used in the East for centuries, but are only now becoming readily available in the West.

Dublin Bay Prawn Cocktail

This homage to the classic appetizer of the '60s is actually a very simple but attractive dish that can be made with any type of large prawn, like tigers, or small langoustine. It is very light and makes a very healthy alternative to eating prawns or shrimp with mayonnaise or butter.

It is essential that you get the grill or broiler really very hot, so the shellfish cook quickly. However, be sure they don't get overcooked, or they become dry and tough in a matter of seconds.

If using wooden skewers, it is advisable to soak them in water first so that they don't catch on fire during cooking.

serves 2

6 fresh Dublin Bay prawns (see note, right)
vegetable oil, for brushing
sea salt and freshly ground black pepper
Spicy Lemon Dressing (page 242)
sprigs of fresh shiso leaves (see page 253), for garnish

1   Carefully peel the shell away from each raw Dublin Bay prawn, leaving just the tail fan.

2   Push a bamboo or wooden skewer through the whole length of each prawn, starting at the fan end (this will keep it straight during cooking).

3   Heat a grill or broiler until good and hot. Brush the prawns with a little oil and season with salt and pepper.

4   Quickly cook the prawns on the grill or under the broiler for 2 to 3 minutes, taking care not to overcook them or they will toughen.

5   Arrange 3 of the skewers in a martini glass or similar, and drench with Spicy Lemon Dressing. Garnish each glass with a sprig of the shiso leaves and serve.

note   Dublin Bay prawns are not actually prawns, but what the French call *langoustines*, the Spanish call *langoustino*, and the Italians *scampi*. They are, in fact, very small members of the lobster family and have delicious sweet flesh with a flavor that is like that of the very best lobster meat.

Nobu Ceviche, Greek-Style

This version of a traditional Greek salad is one that we make at our restaurant on the Greek island of Mykonos. The vegetables and feta cheese both go really well with our Ceviche Sauce and the salad is, of course, best served in summer. You can use any variety or color of tomatoes that are available, as long as they are good and ripe.

serves 4

12 cooked shrimp, shelled and deveined
3 plum tomatoes, cut into 3/4-inch dice
5 ounces feta cheese, cut into 3/4-inch dice
2 teaspoons salt-packed capers, rinsed
1 tablespoon chopped fresh cilantro, plus some whole sprigs
  for garnish
1 small red onion, thinly sliced
1/4 cucumber, cut into 3/4-inch dice

dressing
3 tablespoons Ceviche Sauce (page 247)
1 tablespoon extra-virgin olive oil

1   Put all the salad ingredients in a large salad bowl.

2   Add the Ceviche Sauce and the olive oil, and very gently mix together.

3   Garnish with a few sprigs of cilantro and serve.

note   Only dress the salad at the very last minute before serving it, or it will wilt the vegetables and cause the cheese to break up.

Fresh Egg Roll with Lobster

These fresh egg rolls are simply a salad wrapped in rice paper. They should be made just before they are to be eaten. When working with the rice paper disks, try not to let them get too wet or they will become difficult to handle and tear easily.

serves 4

dressing
1 tablespoon Thai fish sauce (nam pla)
1 tablespoon water
2 tablespoons grapeseed oil
1 tablespoon fresh lemon juice
1 tablespoon chopped rinsed salt-packed capers, plus extra whole capers, for garnish
shichimi togarashi (see page 252)
freshly ground black pepper

1 cooked lobster, about 1 pound
8 rice paper disks, about 6 inches in diameter
8 Chinese cabbage leaves, finely shredded
¼ cucumber, finely diced
rinsed salt-packed capers, for garnish

1   Make the dressing by whisking the first 5 ingredients together, and season with a pinch of shichimi togarashi and a generous twist of black pepper.

2   Remove the cooked lobster from its shell, rinse well, pat dry, and cut into rough 1¼-inch strips.

3   To assemble the egg rolls, lay a damp cloth on a flat work surface, then dip a circle of rice paper into warm water and place it on the damp cloth.

4   Place one-eighth of the shredded cabbage, lobster strips, and cucumber in the middle of the rice paper.

5   Fold the bottom edges of the rice paper over the top of the filling and then roll it over to encase the filling. Fold the right and then the left edges in toward the middle and finish by rolling it into a cylinder. Make 7 more rolls in the same way.

6   Serve the rolls garnished with some whole capers, if you like, with the dressing in a separate bowl. Dip the rolls in the dressing to eat them.

note   To cook your own lobster, see page 59. When buying already-cooked lobster, check that they are a bright red-orange color, have a fresh aroma, and that the tail section will spring back into a curled position after being straightened out. When shelling, all the lobster is edible, except for the small stomach (hard sac) behind the head and the dark intestinal vein running down the back of the tail, so remove and discard these.

Oysters with Mint and Cucumber Salsa

The freshness of the mint in the salsa makes a surprisingly good foil for the oysters.

serves 2

6 fresh oysters
crushed ice, to serve

salsa
2 tablespoons finely diced cucumber
2 tablespoons finely chopped red onion
1/4 cup Ponzu (page 248)
1 tablespoon chopped fresh mint

carrot and cucumber shavings, for garnish

1   Open the oysters (see page 40) and turn each one over in its curved half-shell. Arrange on a bed of crushed ice in a suitable serving dish.

2   Make the salsa by mixing all the ingredients together.

3   Spoon a little of the salsa over the top of each oyster and serve immediately

4   Garnish the dish with some carrot and cucumber shavings for added color, and 1 or 2 of the discarded top shells.

note   When making the salsa, only add the mint once you are ready to serve the oysters, as it will turn brown if left in the salsa for any time.

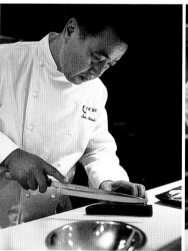

Mussels with Matsuhisa Salsa

The salsa and the red chili slices give the mussels a really spicy zing, making this a great dish to serve as finger food or as an appetizer. The shredded daikon makes an unusual and eye-catching alternative base to the more common crushed ice or sea salt base for cooked mussels.

serves 4

12 to 16 fresh mussels
pinch of salt
shredded daikon (see page 250)
1/2 lime
1 long red chili, cut across into thin slices

Matsuhisa Salsa
1/4 cup finely chopped onion
1 tablespoon soy sauce
6 1/2 tablespoons rice vinegar
1 tablespoon grapeseed oil
1/2 teaspoon chili oil
1/2 teaspoon sea salt
1/4 teaspoon chili-garlic sauce (page 250)
1/4 teaspoon finely grated ginger
2 teaspoons finely chopped fresh parsley

1   First make the salsa. Rinse the onion in cold water to remove the sharpness, then drain well. In a bowl, mix the drained onion with the rest of the ingredients, except the parsley.

2   Wash the mussels under cold running water and check they are clean, removing any beards and discarding any mussels that stay open when tapped.

3   Place the mussels in a steamer with a pinch of salt added to the water and steam for 5 minutes. Remove from the steamer and discard any mussels that haven't opened; let cool a little.

4   Remove the top half of the shell of each mussel and loosen the mussel in the bottom shell with a teaspoon or knife.

5   Arrange on a bed of shredded daikon in a suitable dish, set around a lime half. Stir the parsley into the salsa and spoon a little of it over each mussel. Top each with a slice of red chili.

note   When buying your mussels, allow 2 or 3 more than you need in the event any are dead, in which case they won't close when tapped or won't open when cooked.

Spanish Mackerel Sashimi with Dried Miso

The intense flavor of the dried miso takes the place of salt in this dish and adds a good deal of kick to the mackerel. Spanish mackerel is much larger than the common mackerel, rather more like the tuna, which is a relative of both. It has a very superior flavor. You can, of course, use either tuna or ordinary mackerel for this dish.

makes 5

5 ounces fresh Spanish mackerel, filleted and skinned
1 teaspoon finely chopped garlic
1 teaspoon finely chopped ginger
1 teaspoon Dried Miso (page 249)
freshly ground black pepper
5 Belgian endive leaves
1/2 lime, peeled and peel reserved
finely shredded green onion, for garnish

1   Using a large knife, roughly mince the mackerel fillet, but do not chop so much that it turns into a paste; place it in a bowl.

2   Add the garlic, ginger, and half the dried miso, and season with a little black pepper; then very gently mix everything together.

3   Spoon the mackerel mixture into the middle of the Belgian endive leaves, then arrange them around the lime half on a serving dish. Sprinkle with the rest of the dried miso and place some of the shredded green onion on the top of each leaf. Arrange the lime peel on the lime half to complete the garnish.

note   When eating, squeeze a little of the juice from the lime over the tops.

Beef Tataki

The tataki principle of quickly searing the beef on the outside in a very hot pan gives a wonderful texture, taste, and color contrast between the raw middle and the seared outside. The well-browned and caramelized exterior of the beef also develops more flavor in the rest of the beef by imbuing it with a gentle, sweet smokiness. For this sort of quick treatment where most of the beef remains raw, you do, of course, have to use the very best beef.

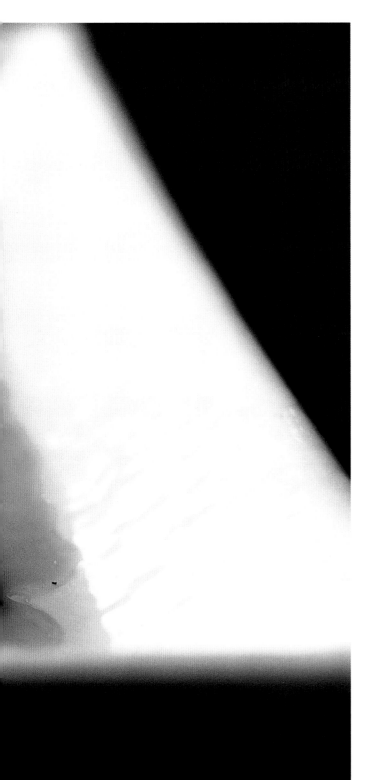

serves 4

Tosa-Zu Sauce
5 tablespoons soy sauce
1/2 cup rice vinegar
1/3 cup dried bonito flakes (see page 250)

ice cubes
7 ounces tenderloin of beef
freshly ground black pepper
vegetable oil, for deep-frying
2 or 3 cloves garlic, thinly sliced
2 tablespoons thinly sliced green onion

1   First make the sauce. Warm the soy sauce and vinegar slightly in a small saucepan, taking care not to let the mixture boil, then add the dried bonito flakes. Cool to room temperature and then strain out the bonito flakes.

2   Have ready a bowl of ice water. Season the beef with black pepper and heat a dry nonstick skillet until very hot. Sear each surface of the beef for 5 seconds, ensuring all sides are completely seared and no red meat is visible. Plunge the beef into the ice water to stop the cooking process. Remove, pat dry with paper towels, and chill in the refrigerator.

3   Bring about 3/4 inch of oil in a saucepan to 300°F and slowly deep-fry the garlic slices in it until they turn a light golden brown. Remove immediately and drain on paper towels.

4   Thinly slice the beef (1/16 to 1/8 inch thick) and arrange the slices on a flat serving dish.

5   Top each slice of beef with a little of the green onion and a slice of fried garlic. Spoon some of the sauce around the edges of the beef and serve.

hot appetizers

Scallop Chawan Mushi

Chawan mushi is a very delicate, light, stock-enriched egg custard. In Japan it is regarded by many as a soup, even though the egg sets in the steaming process. This dish can also be served cold in the summer; just refrigerate after cooking.

serves 4

3 large eggs
2 cups Dashi (page 17)
2 tablespoons sake
2 tablespoons soy sauce
1/2 teaspoon sea salt
4 large fresh scallops, cleaned and any coral removed
4 teaspoons caviar
fine strips of pared lime peel, for garnish

1   In a bowl, whisk the eggs until smooth, then add the Dashi, sake, soy sauce, and salt. Mix well and strain the mixture through a very fine strainer or cheesecloth.

2   Slice each scallop across its depth to produce 3 or 4 rounds and arrange them overlapping on the bottom of a small bowl suitable for steaming.

3   Carefully pour the egg mixture into each of the bowls and remove any bubbles that have formed on the surface with the edge of some paper towels.

4   Cover the bowls with plastic wrap and very gently steam them for 15 to 20 minutes, until the egg mixture sets. The chawan mushi is done when a toothpick inserted into the middle comes out clean.

5   Remove the plastic wrap and place a teaspoon of caviar on each dish. Garnish with some strips of pared lime peel. Serve with a spoon.

note   Try to buy diver scallops if you can find them, as not only are they usually larger, but they are generally in better condition and they are much more ecologically sound.

Crab Harumaki

Harumaki are a Japanese version of the egg roll. This really delicious combination of tasty fresh crabmeat with shiitake mushrooms and shiso leaves encased in a crispy skin and served with a tangy dipping sauce continues to be a favorite in all the restaurants.

serves 4

Spicy Ponzu Dip
2/3 cup Ponzu (page 248)
2 teaspoons green Tabasco sauce
juice of 1 lime
1 tablespoon finely chopped ginger
1 tablespoon finely chopped red onion
2 teaspoons finely chopped seeded red chili
1 1/2 teaspoons finely chopped fresh cilantro

4 shiitake mushrooms
4 fresh shiso leaves (see page 253), plus extra for garnish
4 egg roll wrappers
7 ounces cooked crab claw meat
salt and freshly ground black pepper
flour, for sealing
vegetable oil, for deep-frying

1   First make the dip by combining all the ingredients together. Mix well and pour into a small dipping bowl.

2   Cut the mushrooms into 1/4-inch slices and halve the shiso leaves.

3   Working with one egg roll wrapper at a time, cut each sheet diagonally in half. Place on a flat surface with the point of its triangle shape facing away from you.

4   Place a shiso leaf half in the middle of each triangle, then one-eighth of the crabmeat on top of that and finish with 2 slices of shiitake mushroom lengthwise on top of the crab. Season with a little salt and freshly ground black pepper.

5   Fold the left side of the wrapper in over the filling toward the middle, followed by the right side. Roll the wrapper up away from you and seal the end with a little flour and water mixture. Care should be taken that the roll is completely sealed at the edges, otherwise the oil will get inside the roll while it is frying.

6   When all the harumaki are made, heat oil for deep-frying to a temperature of 350°F and fry the rolls in the hot oil until golden brown all over. Drain briefly on paper towels. Serve immediately, with the bowl of dip and garnish with more shiso leaves.

note   Any type of egg roll wrappers or wonton skins will do.

Matsuhisa Tiger Prawns, London-Style

These prawns are designed to be eaten in one bite in order to experience the full effect of all of the flavors together—the sweetness of the prawns, the citrus tang of the yuzu, and the saltiness of the caviar. It is very popular as a canapé.

serves 2

5 fresh tiger prawns in the shell, each around 1 ounce
1 tablespoon clarified butter (see page 126)
1 cep (porcini) mushroom, cut into 5 pieces
3 fresh shiso leaves, cut in half lengthwise
2 teaspoons Creamy Spicy Sauce (page 246)
5 teaspoons Oscietra caviar
2 teaspoons yuzu juice (see page 253)

1   To prepare the raw prawns, first remove the heads, then remove the shells, leaving the tail pieces intact. Cut along the back and remove the black intestinal tract or "vein," then rinse under cold water and drain.

2   Make a cut along the length of the back, but not all the way through, to butterfly each prawn. Lightly score lines at 45 degrees across the prawn with the heel of the knife blade to prevent the prawn from curling up too much during cooking.

3   Heat the clarified butter in a skillet and sauté the mushroom until just cooked.

4   Heat the oven to 300°F. On the cut side of each prawn, place a piece of shiso leaf, a piece of cep, and a little of the Creamy Spicy Sauce. Fold the end of the prawn over toward the tail and secure with a wooden toothpick.

5   Bake in the oven for 3 to 4 minutes, until the prawns are just cooked through and opaque. Transfer to a serving dish and top each prawn with a teaspoon of caviar and a little of the yuzu juice.

Oysters with Pancetta

This baked oyster dish is very simple and quick to make, but it is important to ensure the pancetta is sliced very thinly, so the oysters cook quickly.

serves 4

12 fresh rock oysters
1 cup sea salt
white of 1 egg
6 thin slices of pancetta (see above)
1/2 lime, to serve
fresh flat-leaf parsley leaves, for garnish

1   Remove the oysters from their shells (see note below) and rinse with cold water, then drain well.

2   Wash the bottom (curved) halves of the shells to remove any sand or shell debris and wipe dry with paper towels.

3   Heat the oven to 350°F. Mix the salt with the egg white to use as a base for the shells to bake on. Arrange 12 little piles on a baking dish suitable for serving from around the lime half, then place a cleaned shell on top of each mound.

4   Cut the pancetta slices in half and wrap each oyster in a piece. Place each on a prepared shell.

5   Bake in the oven for 3 to 4 minutes and serve while still hot, with the lime ball in the center of the dish and each shell garnished with a parsley leaf.

note   To open an oyster, place your thumb about half an inch from the end of the oyster knife to prevent it from sliding along the oyster shell, and insert the blade in between the two valves at one side of the muscle "hinge" at the back of the shell. Wedge the knife into the "hinge" to cut through the muscle from the side. Lift or twist the knife to open the shell.

Whelks, "Escargot-Style"

This is an adaptation of the classic French *escargots à la bourguignonne*, but using sea snails—which is what whelks are. Only the small amount of soy sauce and the pinch of shichimi togarashi differentiate from the traditional garlic and shallot butter used to stuff the creatures.

serves 4

Garlic and Parsley Butter
1³/4 sticks butter
4 cloves garlic, finely chopped
2¹/2 cups finely chopped fresh flat-leaf parsley
¹/3 cup finely chopped shallot
2 teaspoons soy sauce
juice of 1 lemon
sea salt and freshly ground black pepper
pinch of shichimi togarashi (see page 252)

8 large fresh live whelks

to serve
sea salt
egg white

1   To make the flavored butter, allow the butter to soften at room temperature and mix in the rest of the ingredients.

2   Scrub the whelks with a scourer under cold running water. Place in a large pan of boiling salted water and cook for 5 minutes, then drain and leave to cool.

3   Remove the whelk meat from the shell with a skewer. Turning the shell while doing this makes it easier to extract all of the meat; cut away the guts and discard. Rinse the meat and the shells to remove any sand, then chop the meat into large pieces, place back in the shells, and pack with the butter mixture.

4   Heat the oven to 400°F and crumple some foil into a pillow shape on a baking sheet (this helps prevent the shells falling over). Place the shells carefully on it, so when the butter melts, it remains in the shell. Bake for 10 to 12 minutes, until the butter is bubbling.

5   Serve on a bed of salt mixed with a little egg white, which keeps them upright.

note   Although whelks are available all year, they are at their best in the summer months.

Scallops with Spicy Black Bean Sauce

The scallops are baked in their shells with a little sake and some black bean paste, which create a sauce in the bottom of the shell.

serves 2

2 large fresh, live scallops
2/3 cup thinly shredded cabbage
1/3 cup thinly shredded leek
1/4 cup Spicy Black Bean Sauce (page 246)
freshly ground black pepper

to serve
sea salt
egg white

1   Heat the oven to 400°F. Scrub the outside of the scallop shells. Then, using a knife, open the scallop shells and extract the scallop meat. Remove the beard and the frilly outer membrane from each scallop muscle and discard. Scrub the inside of the deepest shell from each scallop and pat dry.

2   Nestle the scallops in the middle of the cleaned shells and arrange the shredded cabbage and leek around the outside of the scallops. Spoon the black bean sauce over the top of the scallops and season with pepper.

3   Bake in the oven for 6 to 8 minutes, until the scallops are just cooked through.

4   Serve on a bed of salt mixed with a little egg white, which keeps them upright.

note   If you can't get fresh scallops in their shells, use any shelled fresh scallop and cook them in an earthenware baking dish.

Spicy Quail Tempura

In this recipe, the quail is first dipped in soy milk and then in seasoned flour, to give the outside a lovely, crunchy texture. The quail can be eaten with fingers, holding it by the bones.

serves 2

1 whole dressed quail
vegetable oil, for deep-frying
¹/2 lime
Red Anticucho Sauce (page 246)

coating
¹/2 cup flour
¹/2 teaspoon cayenne pepper
2 teaspoons dried oregano
1 teaspoon ground cumin
¹/2 teaspoon salt
1 teaspoon freshly ground black pepper
3 tablespoons soy milk

1 Remove the legs and the breasts of the quail from the carcass, then remove the thigh bones from the legs, leaving the drumsticks. Clean the ends of the wing bones and drumsticks by scraping with a knife, which ensures they don't become too dark while frying.

2 Make the coating by mixing together all the ingredients except the soy milk.

3 Heat oil for deep-frying to 350°F. Dip the quail legs and breasts into the soy milk and then into the seasoned flour, making sure they are well coated with the mixture.

4 Deep-fry the legs first for 30 seconds, then add the breasts and continue to fry both for 3 minutes longer, or until just cooked. Remove with a slotted spoon and drain on paper towels.

5 Arrange on a serving dish accompanied by quarters of lime and a cup of the dipping sauce.

note Tempura items needn't always be cooked in batter, but can be coated in this simple way with seasoned flour. This treatment works equally well with other small birds, such as squab.

Foie Gras with Mustard Miso and Butternut Squash Chips

Here the sweet flavor of the squash and the mustard in the miso give another dimension to freshly sautéed foie gras.

serves 4

1 small butternut squash
vegetable oil, for deep-frying
7 ounces fresh duck foie gras, at room temperature
sea salt and freshly ground black pepper
2 tablespoons Mustard Miso (page 247)
fresh flat-leaf parsley leaves, for garnish

1   Cut off the top cylindrical part of the squash and peel it, making sure all the outside skin is completely removed. Slice the squash cylinder as thinly as possible into disks about 1/16 inch thick.

2   Bring a pan of oil 1 1/2 inches deep to 300°F and fry the squash disks a few at a time, until golden and crisp, then drain on paper towels. Care should be taken when frying the squash so the chips do not become too dark in color.

3   Slice the foie gras into eight 3/4-ounce pieces about 1/2 inch thick. Season these with salt and pepper and sauté in a very hot, dry skillet for 1 minute on each side, then drain on paper towels.

4   To assemble, place a piece of foie gras on each squash chip and drizzle a little flavored miso over each one, then top with a parsley leaf. Serve immediately on a flat dish, as the squash chips will become soft if left for too long.

note   When frying foie gras, it must be done very fast in a very hot, dry pan, otherwise it will just melt.

Pimientos de Padrón

Named after the town of Padrón in the Spanish province of Galicia, these wonderful small sweet green peppers are very much like their Japanese cousin, the shishito pepper. About one in every twelve or so of these little fellows is actually hot and this makes it fun when eating to see who gets the heat. These can be either broiled or fried. Sprinkled with a little sea salt, they make an excellent start to a meal.

serves 2

12 pimientos de Padrón
sea salt

1   Heat a hot broiler or barbecue grill.

2   Place 6 peppers on 2 parallel bamboo skewers. Using 2 skewers in this way stops the peppers rotating on the skewer while cooking so they cook evenly. Do the same with the other peppers.

3   Place the racks of peppers on the hot broiler or grill and cook for 1 to 2 minutes, until the skins begin to blister and the peppers become slightly soft.

4   Sprinkle with sea salt and serve while still hot.

note   When using bamboo skewers on a barbecue, it is a good idea to soak them in water beforehand, to help prevent them from charring over the heat.

salads

Turnip Salad with Scallops

This is very simple to prepare and makes a really attractive finished dish. The contrast between the textures of the crisp vegetables and the soft scallops makes for an interesting combination, which is then accentuated by the sharp citrus kick of the dressing.

serves 4

Yuzu Ponzu Dressing
2 tablespoons Yuzu Dressing (page 63)
2 tablespoons Ponzu (page 248)

6 baby turnips
6 large radishes
4 large fresh scallops, shelled
^{1}/$_2$ lime
pinch of sea salt

1　To make the dressing, combine the Yuzu Dressing and Ponzu and mix well.

2　Slice the turnips and radishes very thinly (about ^{1}/$_{32}$ inch) lengthwise on a mandoline and set aside.

3　Slice the scallops into thin disks, trying to get as many slices as you can from each scallop.

4　Arrange alternating slices of radish and turnip around the edge of a serving plate, making sure each slice overlaps the previous one, and continue until the circle is complete.

5　Repeat the same process again, only this time make the circle smaller in the middle and alternate slices of scallop, radish, and turnip, so the slices begin to resemble the petals of a flower.

6　Place the lime half in the middle, sprinkle the dish with sea salt, and then carefully pour the sauce over the top of the salad.

notes　Try to find the smallest baby turnips you can, so the outside skin won't require peeling. A mandoline grater is essential for this dish, preferably a Japanese mandoline, to get the slices as thin as possible.

If you can, get radishes with some of their green stems still attached and slice with some of these still on for an even more attractive presentation.

Crabmeat and Punterella Salad with Spicy Lemon and Caper Dressing

Punterella is a delicious salad green that is very popular in Italy. It has a rather bitter taste, resembling that of Belgian endive (it is often called "wild Belgian endive"), which is actually quite addictive. In this very simple recipe, we combine white crabmeat and a zesty lemon dressing to make a perfect accompaniment to the punterella.

serves 4

1 head of punterella
5 tablespoons Spicy Lemon Dressing (page 242)
2 tablespoons chopped rinsed salt-packed capers
7 ounces cooked white crabmeat

1   Rinse the punterella well and remove and discard the thick head and stems, keeping the smaller tender pieces. Place these in a mixing bowl and dress with 3 tablespoons of the Spicy Lemon Dressing; toss well to coat.

2   Arrange the dressed punterella on a serving dish, sprinkle the capers and crabmeat on top, and dress again with the remaining 2 tablespoons of dressing.

note   You can use any bitter salad leaf, such as Belgian endive, frisée, or radicchio, if punterella is not available.

Lobster and Watercress Salad with Watercress Dressing

The combination of fresh lobster and peppery watercress, together with the crunch of black sesame seeds, makes this a satisfying and very refreshing salad.

serves 4 to 6

1 live lobster (about 12 ounces)
1 large bunch of watercress
2 teaspoons black sesame seeds
1/2 yellow bell pepper, seeded and cut into fine strips, for garnish

Watercress Dressing
1 bunch of watercress
6 1/2 tablespoons rice vinegar
5 tablespoons grapeseed oil
2 teaspoons sea salt
1 teaspoon freshly ground black pepper

1   Put the lobster in the freezer for about 20 minutes, so it goes into a deep sleep and won't be aware of the next stage.

2   Bring a saucepan of salted water large enough to cover the lobster to a boil. Plunge the lobster headfirst into the water, bring back to a boil, and simmer for 6 minutes. Remove the lobster and plunge it into a bowl of ice water to cool.

3   Remove the tail and claws from the body and crack the shell from the meat. Cut the meat into bite-size slices.

4   To make the salad, remove the thicker stems (which should be saved for the dressing) from the watercress, then roughly chop and place in a mixing bowl.

5   To make the dressing, pick all the leaves and smaller stems from the watercress and combine all the larger stems together with the reserved stems from the other bunch. Blanch the large stems in boiling salted water for 30 seconds, then refresh in ice water. Drain and chop together with the leaves and smaller stems. Add all the remaining dressing ingredients to a blender and blend together, adding the chopped blanched stems and leaves a little at a time until smooth.

6   Add a small amount of dressing to the watercress in the mixing bowl, sprinkle with a little of the black sesame seeds, and mix gently.

7   Place the salad to one side of the middle of a serving dish and spoon the remaining dressing around the edge, then arrange the lobster pieces to the side of the salad.

8   Garnish the salad with the slices of yellow pepper and sprinkle everything with more black sesame seeds.

note   The dressing should be made and used at the last minute, as the vinegar quickly turns the watercress brown.

Salmon Tataki with Paper-Thin Salad

Using paper-thin slices of baby vegetables instead of salad leaves gives this dish an interesting twist. The vegetables are first plunged into ice-cold water to give them a crunchy texture that contrasts nicely with the seared salmon sashimi.

serves 4

7 ounces boneless, skinless fresh salmon fillets
freshly ground black pepper
Jalapeño Dressing (page 242)

Paper-Thin Salad
2 baby beets
2 baby carrots
2 baby green zucchini
2 baby yellow zucchini
2 baby turnips
4 red radishes
bowlfuls of ice water

1   Heat a nonstick skillet until medium-hot. Season the salmon fillets with black pepper, then sear them for 5 seconds on each side. Make sure all the outside is completely seared and turns white. Immediately plunge them into ice water to stop the cooking process. Drain and pat dry with paper towels, then refrigerate.

2   To prepare the salad, keeping the beets to one side, slice the baby vegetables lengthwise very thinly (about $1/32$ inch thick) on a mandoline grater into a bowl of ice water. Leave them in the ice water for 1 hour; this will cause them to tighten up and become crunchy. Repeat the same process with the beets, but place the slices in a separate bowl of water, to stop the color from running into the other vegetables, and rinse until the water becomes clear; then add some ice to chill. You might want to wear disposable gloves for this, to prevent staining your hands.

3   Drain the baby vegetables and the beets separately, then mix them together.

4   Pour some of the dressing on the bottom of a serving dish, so it completely covers the bottom.

5   Cut the chilled seared salmon into slices about $1/4$ inch thick and arrange across the middle of the plate, then place the vegetable salad in the middle on top of the salmon.

Tomatillo and Gooseneck Barnacle Salad

Gooseneck barnacles, also known as percebes, are almost prehistoric in appearance and grow in clumps on rocky shores all around the Atlantic. They are particularly revered in Spain and Portugal, where they are eaten quickly steamed or even raw. They have been farmed in Washington state for a decade or so, and may be found in speciality fish markets. They have a slightly sweet flavor with an exquisitely strong taste of the sea, and here this is complemented by the gently acidic taste of the tomatillos. Also known as the Spanish tomato in Mexico, from where it originates, the tomatillo resembles a green tomato, so you can use these if you can't find any tomatillos.

serves 4

1 pound fresh percebes
sea salt
bowl of ice water
2 tomatillos
4 radishes

Yuzu Dressing
1/2 cup plus, 1 tablespoon yuzu juice (see page 253)
2 tablespoons soy sauce
1/3 teaspoon freshly ground black pepper
1/2 teaspoon finely chopped garlic
6 tablespoons grapeseed oil

1   Blanch the percebes in boiling salted water for 1 minute, then refresh in ice water. When cold, peel them by pinching the outer tube just below the "hoof-shaped" plates and prying it off with your fingernails. This will reveal the pinkish-white, fleshy, tubelike neck inside, which can be pulled or cut off. This is the edible portion of the percebes. Discard the outer skin and "hooves."

2   Make the dressing by mixing all the ingredients together.

3   Slice the tomatillos and radishes thinly and arrange on a serving dish, alternating each slice to form a circle in the middle of the dish. Arrange the percebes in the middle and drench with about half the yuzu dressing (keep the rest in the refrigerator for another seafood salad, like the Turnip Salad with Scallops on page 55).

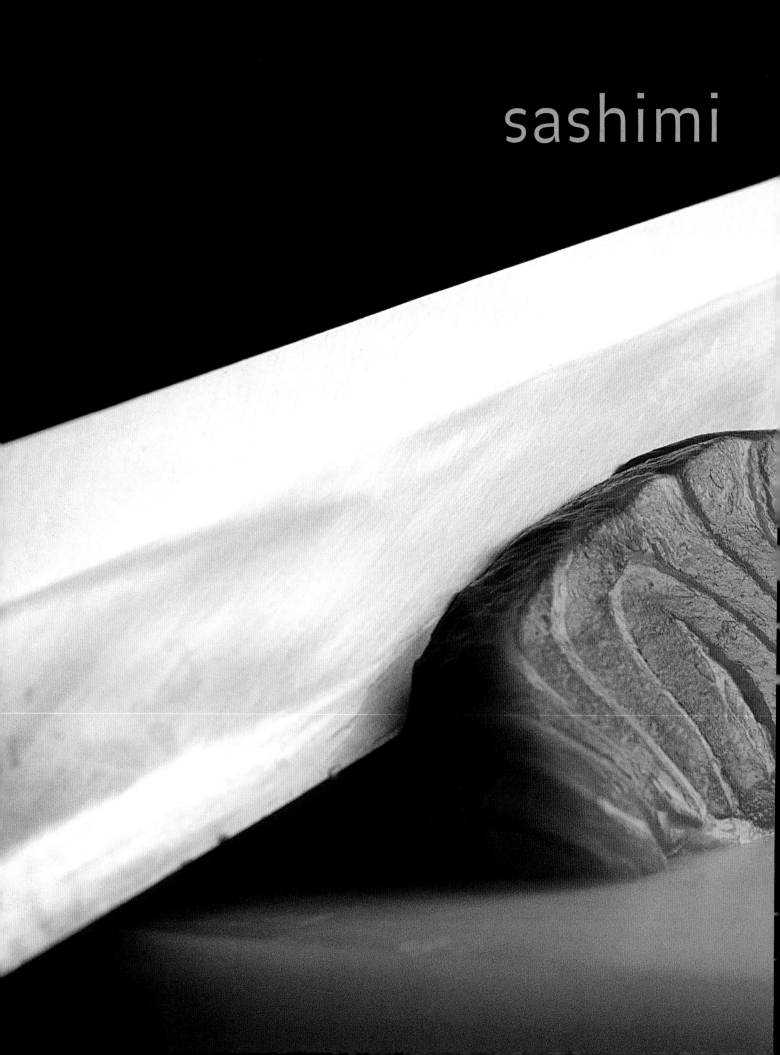

sashimi

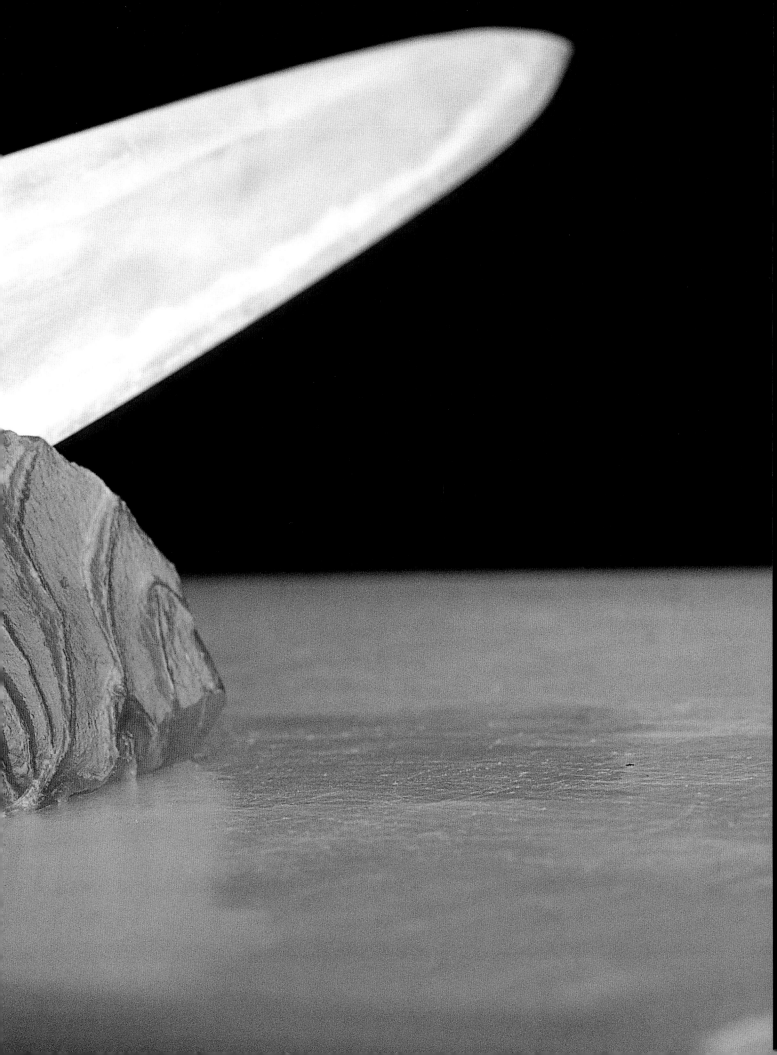

Lobster Carpaccio

In this dish, the raw lobster is sliced very thinly and hot olive oil is poured over the top. This releases the delicate flavors of the lobster and the aromas of ginger and garlic.

serves 4

1 small live lobster, 7 to 10 ounces
1/2 clove garlic, smashed to a paste with the flat of a knife
1 tablespoon finely shredded ginger
1 tablespoon snipped fresh chives
sea salt and freshly ground black pepper
1 tablespoon Yuzu Dressing (page 63)
small quantity of extra-virgin olive oil
a few green olives, halved
a few fresh tatsoi leaves (see page 253)

1   Put the lobster in the freezer for about 20 minutes, so it goes into a deep sleep and won't be aware of the next stage.

2   Bring a saucepan of salted water large enough to cover the lobster to a boil. Plunge the lobster headfirst into the water for 30 seconds, remove, and plunge into a bowl of ice water to cool. This enables the meat to be easily removed from the shell.

3   Remove the tail and claws from the body and carefully crack the shells and gently remove the tail and claw meat. Slice the tail meat into medallions about 1/4 inch thick; cut the claw meat into 1/4-inch-thick slices and keep separate.

4   Lay a large piece of plastic wrap on a chopping board and lay the tail medallions on top of the plastic wrap, leaving a little space in between each slice. Cover with another large piece of plastic wrap.

5   With a meat mallet, gently bat out each tail slice as thinly as possible, 1/16 to 1/32 inch, taking care not to tear holes in the meat. Peel away the top layer of plastic wrap by holding down on each flattened piece one at a time until the plastic wrap is removed.

6   Place the lobster meat still attached to the bottom layer of plastic wrap on the middle of the serving plate with the plastic wrap uppermost. Gently peel away the plastic wrap, again holding down each flattened piece of meat so all the flattened lobster medallions are left on the plate.

7   Dab the medallions with a little of the garlic puree and sprinkle the ginger and the snipped chives evenly on top. Season with a little sea salt and freshly ground black pepper, then drizzle the dressing over the top.

8   Heat the olive oil in a small pan until it just begins to smoke, then pour it over the lobster slices to sear the top. Garnish the middle with the sliced claws, some green olive halves on top of those, and the tatsoi leaves.

Octopus Carpaccio

This is a novel way to serve octopus and makes an attractive finished dish. The octopus is cooked and the tentacles are pressed together to form a sausage, which is then sliced and dressed with dried miso, olive oil, and lemon juice.

serves 4

1 fresh Atlantic or Mediterranean octopus
1 teaspoon fresh lemon juice
1 tablespoon olive oil
1 1/2 teaspoons snipped fresh chives
1 teaspoon Dried Miso (page 249)

1   To prepare the octopus, pound the tentacles with the end of a wooden mallet to help tenderize the meat. Next cut a slit around the beak of the octopus (found in the middle of where the tentacles join the head) and remove the beak. Turn the head of the octopus inside out and remove all the innards and the eggs, if any. Rinse well under cold running water and remove any sinews in the head with a knife. Turn the head back out the right way and place in a ceramic mortar. Put your hand inside the head and rub the octopus around the bowl for 5 to 10 minutes, to help remove the sliminess, which appears like beaten egg white in the bowl, and any sand that is in the tentacles. (Salt could be added at this stage to speed the process up, but it will toughen the flesh.) When all the slime has gone, rinse well under cold running water again, not forgetting inside the head.

2   Fill a saucepan with enough water to cover the octopus, salt it generously (2 tablespoons salt to each quart of water), bring to a boil, and slowly place the octopus in the water, tentacles first. Bring back to a boil, cover, and reduce the heat to a slow simmer; then simmer for 30 to 40 minutes, depending on the size of the octopus, until tender.

3   When cooked, remove the octopus from the water and cut off the 8 tentacles where they join the head—this should be done while it is still fairly hot. While the tentacles are still warm, spread a piece of plastic wrap on a bamboo mat and lay the tentacles side by side, alternating the thick and thin ends on each side. The roll needs to be about 2 1/4 inches in diameter (if the tentacles are very large and they are too big to roll up in the mat, make a second mat). Roll up the mat and tie tightly with string, then place in the freezer while still warm.

4   Just before it begins to freeze, after about 20 minutes, remove the roll from the freezer and place in the refrigerator.

5   To serve, unwrap the octopus roll and cut across into slices 1 1/4 to 2 inches thick. Serving 2 or 3 slices per person, arrange on serving plates and dress with the lemon juice and olive oil, then scatter with the snipped chives and dried miso.

notes   An average whole octopus, as here, will produce 4 portions, and you can chop the head into bite-size pieces and serve with the Ceviche Sauce on page 247.
Rolling the octopus while still hot will help the tentacles stick together because of their gelatin content. The more the tentacles are pounded at the beginning, the more tender the finished result will be. Octopus usually requires salt, but here the dried miso takes its place.

Dublin Bay Prawn Sashimi

Dublin Bay prawns, also known as langoustines, scampi, or Norwegian lobsters, have a wonderful sweet shellfish taste. Here we prepare them very simply to retain as much of the natural flavors as possible. Only live langoustines should be used for this dish to ensure the utmost freshness.

serves 1

2 live Dublin Bay prawns
1/2 lemon
2 tablespoons olive oil
sea salt and freshly ground black pepper
chive stems, for garnish

1   Put the Dublin Bay prawns in the freezer for about 15 minutes, so they go into a deep sleep and won't be aware of the next stage.

2   Blanch the prawns for 10 seconds in boiling, salted water and then plunge them into ice water to cool them down and stop the cooking process; drain well.

3   With a large knife, cut right through the head and body, then cut through the tail, leaving the underside of the tail shell intact so the prawn opens in half like a book, and the soft underside of the tail shell is still joined together in the middle.

4   Lay the opened-out prawns on a serving dish and squeeze the lemon juice over the tail meat, followed by the olive oil. Season with salt and freshly ground black pepper, and garnish with chive stems.

Fresh Octopus Sashimi with Bottarga

In this dish, the texture and flavor of raw octopus are enhanced by the saltiness of the bottarga (see the note opposite) and the citrus juices. For a more detailed description of how to prepare octopus, see page 68.

Here, the suckers removed from the octopus's tentacles are used as an unusual and eye-catching garnish. You need to clean these very carefully, too, as described and shown opposite, because they can be very sandy.

serves 4

1 large fresh octopus tentacle
a little sea salt
1 piece of mullet bottarga (see note below)
4 asparagus spears, peeled and blanched
1/2 teaspoon salt-packed baby capers, rinsed
1/4 teaspoon crushed black peppercorns
1 teaspoon yuzu juice (see page 253)
1 teaspoon fresh lemon juice
1 teaspoon freshly ground black pepper

1 Remove the suckers from the octopus tentacle by cutting from the thickest end just below the skin. As you work the knife sideways, gradually remove the skin underneath the suckers along the length of the tentacle, then repeat the process for the remaining skin left all around the tentacle.

2 Place the skin with the suckers attached in a mortar and knead with a little salt to remove the slime and sand from inside the suckers.

3 Bring a pan of water with a pinch of salt to a boil and place the suckers in it. Boil for 5 minutes, remove, and drain. Cut the suckers out of the skin and reserve.

4 Using a clean kitchen cloth, gently rub the membrane off the skinned tentacle, then rinse it quickly in cold, salted water and pat dry.

5 Slice the tentacle as thinly as possible, 1/16 to 1/8 inch thick, then slice the bottarga even more thinly. (The bottarga is easier to slice.)

6 Cut the asparagus spears to the same length as the octopus slices and if they are more than 1/4 inch thick, cut each in half lengthwise.

7 Arrange "sandwiches" consisting of a slice of asparagus followed by a slice of octopus, then a slice of bottarga, making sure they overlap one another. Repeat this process to make 8 "sandwiches" in total.

8 Place a reserved sucker on each slice of octopus, then sprinkle the capers, cracked black pepper, and sea salt over the tops. Mix the yuzu juice and lemon juice together, and drizzle this over the tops.

note Bottarga (sometimes called the poor man's caviar) is the roe of the gray mullet (or tuna), which has been pressed and cured in sea salt for a few weeks. It is very popular in the Mediterranean, as well as in Japan, and you might find it in Italian delis as well as Japanese food stores.

Turbot Sashimi with Fried Garlic, Onion, Jalapeño, and Matsuhisa Dressing

The turbot sashimi is dressed with an interesting range of onion textures, from the soft sweet onions in the Matsuhisa Dressing to the chopped red onion and crispy garlic chips on the top.

serves 4

vegetable oil, for deep-frying
2 to 3 cloves garlic, thinly sliced
5 ounces boneless, skinless fresh turbot fillet
1 tablespoon finely chopped red onion
1 teaspoon finely chopped seeded jalapeño pepper
Matsuhisa Dressing (page 242)

1   Bring about $3/4$ inch of oil in a saucepan to 300°F and slowly deep-fry the garlic slices until they turn a light golden brown. Remove immediately and drain on paper towels.

2   On a chopping board, place the turbot fillet with the skinned side up and the tail on the knife-hand side. Steadying the tail end with the fingers of the other hand, hold the knife so the top is inclined sharply to the side away from the fish. Then, from the tail end, start cutting thin slices ($1/16$ to $1/8$ inch thick), keeping the blade at an acute angle to achieve a clean cut across the grain. Try to cut each slice of fish in one drawing stroke, letting the weight of the knife do the work as you pull back the blade.

3   Arrange the slices on a serving dish (you will need about 16 slices for 4 people) and spread the garlic chips across the top, followed by the red onion and the jalapeño. Pour a little of the dressing around the edges of the fish to finish.

note   This method of cutting the fish is called the *Usu Zukuri* technique in Japan, and can be used for any firm white fish, such as snapper, sea bass, and flounder. Obviously, be sure to have a really sharp knife for this and be careful with it when cutting the fish.

Umamijime Tiradito

Here turbot has been marinated with both bonito and konbu to add lots more umami flavor to the raw fish. Lemon and yuzu juices then impart a wonderful citrus tang, and the chili gives it bite.

serves 4

1 sheet of konbu (see page 251)
handful of bonito flakes (see page 250)
2 teaspoons sea salt
1 jalapeño pepper, seeded and finely chopped
5 ounces boneless, skinless fresh turbot fillet
handful of fresh cilantro, stems removed
rocoto chili paste (see page 252) or red chili paste
2 tablespoons fresh lemon juice
1 tablespoon yuzu juice (see page 253)

1 The day before, soak the konbu in cold water for 2 hours. Drain the soaked konbu and wipe it dry with a clean cloth, then cut it in half.

2 Mix the bonito flakes, salt, and jalapeño together and spread over both sides of the turbot. Place the fillet on top of one of the pieces of konbu, then put the other half sheet over the top to make a sandwich with the turbot in the middle. Wrap in plastic wrap and refrigerate overnight.

3 The next day, unwrap the turbot "sandwich," remove the konbu, and reserve. On a chopping board, place the turbot fillet with the skinned side up and the tail on the knife-hand side. Steadying the tail end with the fingers of the other hand, hold the knife so the top is inclined sharply to the side away from the fish. Then, from the tail end, start cutting thin slices ($1/16$ to $1/8$ inch thick), keeping the blade at an acute angle to achieve a clean cut across the grain. Try to cut each slice of fish in one drawing stroke, letting the weight of the knife do the work as you pull back the blade.

4 Arrange the slices on a serving dish (you will need about 16 slices for 4 people) in a fan shape.

5 Roll the reserved konbu up into a cylinder and cut this across into strips as thinly as possible. Place these neatly at the base of the fanned turbot, then arrange the cilantro leaves in between the konbu and the turbot. Put the tiniest dot of chili paste in the middle of each turbot slice. Mix the lemon and yuzu juices and pour this around the dish to finish.

notes When eating this dish, take a leaf of cilantro and a little konbu and eat with a slice of turbot.
   After the lemon and yuzu juices have been added, the dish must be eaten quickly, as this fish will start to "cook" if left for too long. If you can't find yuzu, use limes.

Toro Miso with Jalapeño Salsa

Here the texture and flavor of the tuna belly are heightened by quickly searing the outside surfaces. The slices are then paired with the sweetness and acidity of a yuzu miso dressing and the kick of salsa.

serves 2

Yuzu Miso Sauce

1/2 ounce yuzu peel (see page 253)
2/3 cup Den Miso (page 244)
about 2 tablespoons rice vinegar

3 ounces boneless, skinless fresh toro (tuna belly) in a block
freshly ground black pepper
2 tablespoons Jalapeño Salsa (page 243)
a few blanched skinned fava beans, for garnish

1 To make the sauce, blend the yuzu peel to a pulp in a food processor and strain off the juice, pressing it to get as much out as you can. Mix this into the miso and then add just enough of the vinegar to get a consistency that will coat the back of a spoon.

2 Season the tuna with black pepper. Heat a nonstick skillet until very hot and quickly sear each side of the tuna, making sure all the outside is completely seared and no red meat is visible. Plunge it immediately into ice water to stop the cooking process, then drain and pat dry with paper towels.

3 Flood the base of a serving dish with the sauce. Slice the tuna across into slices 1/8 to 1/4 inch thick and arrange them overlapping in the middle of the plate. Spoon a little of the salsa over the top and garnish with the fava beans.

notes Be sure to plunge the toro immediately into ice water after searing to prevent it from overcooking.
  To spread a sauce evenly around the base of a plate, put the sauce in the middle and carefully tilt the plate so it runs to the edges.

Toro Hagashi

The beauty of this dish is the melt-in-the-mouth toro hagashi, which is essentially the flesh that is found in between the sinews of the tuna meat. This is quickly seared on one side and served with a medley of mushrooms, olives, and capers.

serves 2

3 1/2 ounces fresh toro (tuna belly)
sea salt and freshly ground black pepper
1 teaspoon garlic puree
2 cep (porcini) mushrooms, sliced
4 morels, halved
olive oil, for cooking
4 caper berries
2 pitted green olives, sliced
1 tablespoon fresh green peas, blanched
a little Yuzu Dressing (page 63)

1 From a piece of toro (tuna belly), remove the outer sinew on both sides as illustrated below. Season the tuna with sea salt and black pepper and rub one side with a little garlic puree.

2 Heat a nonstick skillet until medium-hot and quickly sear the garlic-rubbed side of the tuna. Remove from the pan and keep to one side.

3 In the same skillet over medium heat, sauté the cep and morel mushrooms in a little olive oil until just cooked and soft.

4 Add the caper berries, olives, and peas, and toss for 30 seconds. Season with salt and pepper.

5 Place the tuna in the middle of a serving dish and neatly spoon the mushroom mixture over the top. Dress with a little dressing to finish. This dish is best served slightly warm.

note As the toro hagashi meat is very thin, make sure it is quickly seared and removed from the heat, to retain the raw top side.

Duck Tataki with Wasabi Salsa

Most people in the West associate sashimi with raw fish and seafood. In this dish, however, duck breast is seared to make the skin crispy and then given a fiery lift with a wasabi salsa and finished with vinegary ponzu. For the right results, when choosing duck for this dish, do not use wild or well-hung birds—the meat should be very red and fresh.

serves 4

1 leek, trimmed and well rinsed
sea salt and freshly ground black pepper
1 fresh duck breast
1 teaspoon salt-packed capers, rinsed
1/3 recipe quantity Ponzu (page 248)
1/2 sharon fruit, thinly sliced

salsa

2 teaspoons wasabi pickle (wasabi zuke, see page 253)
1 tablespoon finely chopped onion
1/2 teaspoon grated garlic
1 tablespoon grapeseed oil

1   Heat the oven to 350°F. Place the leek on a baking sheet and season with a little salt and pepper, then bake for 10 to 12 minutes, until slightly brown on the outside.

2   Trim any excess fat from the duck breast, leaving a thickness of only 1/16 to 1/8 inch. Gently score the remaining fat with a knife horizontally and vertically 1/4 inch apart to produce a crosshatch pattern on the fat. Do not cut through the fat into the meat.

3   Place a nonstick saucepan over medium heat. Season the duck breast with salt and pepper and place it in the pan, skin side down. Cook for 1 minute, using a spatula to press the duck down so all the fat comes in contact with the pan and starts to render and become crisp. Check after 1 minute to see if it is crisp; if not, cook for 30 seconds longer. When crisp, quickly turn the breast over and sear all the remaining surfaces for a few seconds only, then remove the duck from the pan and set aside to cool.

4   To make the salsa, in a small nonreactive bowl, mix together all the ingredients, then season with salt and pepper to taste.

5   Cut the cooled duck breast across into slices about 1/8 inch thick and arrange them, overlapping one another, on a serving dish. Place a little of the wasabi salsa on each slice of duck breast.

6   Cut the leek into 1/4-inch roundels and place one on the top of each slice of duck breast with a caper. Pour a little of the Ponzu around the slices of duck and garnish with a few slices of sharon fruit.

Watercress and Soy Milk Soup

This is a creamy watercress soup that uses soy milk instead of cream. It is, therefore, very light and healthy, as well as being quick to make. In summer it is also good served cold.

serves 4

3 bunches of watercress
2¹/₂ cups Dashi (page 249)
7 ounces unsweetened soy milk
¹/₄ cup light soy sauce
salt and freshly ground black pepper

1 Pick the watercress from the stems and keep them separate, then roughly chop the stems.

2 In a large saucepan, bring the Dashi just to a boil, add the watercress stems, and simmer for 5 minutes.

3 Pour the mixture into a blender and blend until smooth.

4 Strain the mixture back into the saucepan and add the soy milk. Bring the soup to a slow simmer and add the watercress leaves, reserving a few for garnish. Simmer for 3 minutes.

5 Blend again until smooth and strain into a clean saucepan. Bring back to the heat and add the soy sauce, then season to taste with salt and pepper.

6 Ladle into bowls and garnish with a few shredded watercress leaves.

note This treatment works equally well with other strong-tasting greens, such as spinach and sorrel.

Mushroom Soup with Truffle and Jabugo

This delicate clear soup, scented with white truffles and Iberian ham, is first drunk out of small cups. The remaining solid contents are then eaten at the end with chopsticks.

serves 4

stock
3 1/2 cups Dashi (page 249)
1/4 cup sake
1/4 cup light soy sauce
sea salt

1 3/4 ounces shiitake mushrooms
1 3/4 ounces oyster mushrooms
1 3/4 ounces cep (porcini) mushrooms
3/4 ounce Jabugo or other Iberian ham, cut into fine strips
about 1/16 ounce white truffle slices

1   Make the stock by mixing together the Dashi, sake, and soy sauce with sea salt to taste, then warm slowly in a saucepan to dissolve the salt.

2   Divide each of the mushroom types evenly between 4 soup kettles and fill them with the stock mixture.

3   Put the kettles in a large steamer and steam for 12 minutes. This will let the mushroom flavors infuse slowly into the soup.

4   Add the ham and truffle slices to the soup in each kettle and serve.

note   If you don't have soup kettles, you can just make the soup in a saucepan, but the heat must be kept very low and the soup should not boil.

Baked King Crab Soup

King crab is gently cooked in stock, accented by chili-garlic sauce and an assortment of mushrooms, then baked in the oven under a pastry topping. All the wonderful aromas of this soup are released when the pastry top is removed at the table. You'll need 4 suitably sized ovenproof bowls for this.

serves 4

14 ounces puff pastry dough
flour, for dusting
1 3/4 ounces chanterelle mushrooms
1 3/4 ounces shiitake mushrooms
1 3/4 ounces oyster mushrooms
4 large fresh king crab claws, shelled
1 egg, beaten

stock
3 1/2 cups Dashi (page 249)
1/4 cup sake
1/4 cup light soy sauce
2 teaspoons chili-garlic sauce (see page 250)
1/2 teaspoon sea salt

1   Heat the oven to 350°F.

2   Make the stock by mixing all the ingredients together in a saucepan and warm slowly to dissolve the salt.

3   Roll the dough out on a floured surface to a thickness of about 1/8 inch. Using one of the ovenproof bowls as a guide, cut out 4 dough circles to make "lids" for the bowls. These should be large enough to provide a good overhang when in place.

4   Divide the mushrooms evenly between the 4 bowls, place the crab claws on top of the mushrooms, and cover with the stock, leaving a 1/2 to 3/4 inch gap from the top of the bowl.

5   Brush the rims of the bowls with the egg wash. Making sure they overlap the rim sufficiently, place the dough circles over the bowls and seal at the edges by pressing lightly. There is no need to trim too much from the sides, because this will help keep the dough circles tight on the top, so they don't sag into the soup. Brush the dough tops lightly with the egg wash and make a tiny hole in the middle of each to let steam escape. Bake in the oven for 15 to 20 minutes, until the pastry is baked, risen, and golden.

6   Serve just as it is, straight from the oven.

note   Any assortment of mushrooms can be used, just pick your favorites.

Foie Gras Miso Soup

Here, miso soup is enriched with fresh foie gras and black truffles to produce a dish that is hearty and rich, but with a wonderful silky finish.

serves 4

2 ounces fresh foie gras
1³/4 cups Dashi (page 17)
1³/4 ounces white miso (see page 253)
1/2 teaspoon black truffle oil
4 slices of black truffle

1   Place the foie gras in the freezer for 20 minutes to get it nice and firm.

2   In a nonreactive saucepan, bring the Dashi to just below the boiling point and whisk in the miso a little at a time until dissolved.

3   Preferably using a mandoline, shave the chilled foie gras into the thinnest possible slices, so they will liquefy in the soup.

4   Add the foie gras to the soup over the heat and whisk it in.

5   Add the truffle oil and blend the soup in a blender until smooth.

6   Pour into small soup cups and place a slice of truffle on the top of each portion.

note   Once the foie gras has been added to the soup, it should not be kept hot for too long or it will eventually separate.

Iberian Pork Cheek Miso Soup

Pork cheeks are a much favored delicacy in Spain and those from the Iberian black pigs in Jabugo are particularly celebrated, almost as much as the local world-renowned hams. As the muscles in the cheeks are well used, the delicious meat tends to be very tough, so it needs long, slow cooking.

serves 4

braised pork cheeks
4 pork cheeks, preferably from Iberian black pigs
2 cloves garlic, peeled
1/2 teaspoon black peppercorns
3/4-inch piece of ginger, peeled
1 bird's-eye chili
2 tablespoons light soy sauce

soup
13/4 cups Dashi (page 17)
5 tablespoons white miso paste (see page 253)
2 tablespoons sake
8 baby carrots, cooked
8 baby turnips, cooked
1/4 red chili, thinly sliced
1/4 green chili, thinly sliced
shredded daikon (see page 250)

1   Heat the oven to 300°F. Place the pork cheeks in a casserole dish, add the garlic, pepper, ginger, chili, and soy sauce, then cover with cold water. Cover the casserole with a lid or foil and braise in the oven for 1 1/2 to 2 hours, until tender. Leave the cheeks to cool in the liquid, then remove the cheeks and strain the cooking liquid, reserving both.

2   Make the soup by bringing the Dashi and 1 3/4 cups of the reserved cooking liquid to just below a boil and slowly whisk in the white miso paste until it dissolves. Stir in the sake and strain.

3   To serve, cut the cheeks into bite-size pieces and reheat in some of the remaining cooking liquid. Heat the carrots and turnips quickly in boiling water. Divide the pieces of cheek and the vegetables evenly between 4 deep soup bowls and pour the hot miso soup over. Garnish with the sliced red and green chilies and shredded daikon.

note   There are many varieties of miso paste and they all have different levels of saltiness, so add to the soup in small amounts, tasting as you go.

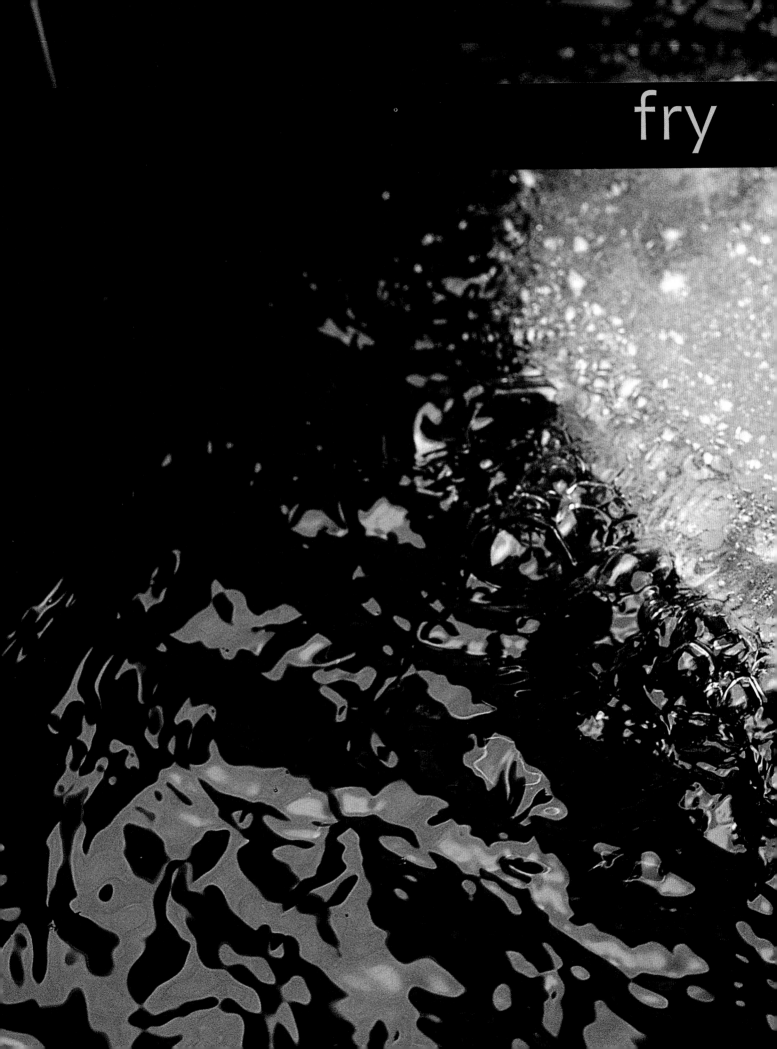

fry

Mediterranean Shrimp Tempura with Jalapeño Ponzu

One of the most popular dishes at all our restaurants is the Rock Shrimp Tempura. Here, we have used the same technique with Mediterranean red shrimp (*crevettes rouges*, *gamberi rossi*), which are large and wonderfully flavored, almost like lobster. They are enlivened by a spicy jalapeño-flavored ponzu.

serves 2

12 fresh Mediterranean red shrimp (see note below)
vegetable oil, for deep-frying
handful of assorted salad leaves
small quantity of Yuzu Dressing (page 63)
1/4 cup Jalapeño Ponzu (page 245)
snipped fresh chives, for garnish

Tempura Batter
7 ounces ice-cold water
1 egg yolk
2/3 cup all-purpose flour

1   Prepare the shrimp by removing the heads from the bodies and peeling the shell from the tails. Cut a small incision along the back of each and remove the dark vein or intestinal tract. Rinse under cold running water and drain.

2   Heat a medium-to-large pan of oil (3 to 4 inches deep) to a temperature of 350°F.

3   To make the tempura batter, in a mixing bowl, mix the ice-cold water and the egg yolk, using a pair of chopsticks. Then add the flour, a little at a time, mixing it in with the chopsticks until it is all incorporated. Don't overwork it, or the batter will be heavy—aim for a loose batter that still has a few little lumps of unmixed flour.

4   In a large bowl, dress the salad leaves with a little of the dressing, then place in a large serving dish. Put the ponzu in a small dipping cup.

5   One at a time, dip the shrimp into the cold tempura batter, then let any excess batter run off. Gently place in the hot oil and fry for 1 to 2 minutes, until lightly colored and crisp. Transfer with a slotted spoon to paper towels to drain.

6   Once all the shrimp are cooked, place them on the salad leaves and sprinkle with snipped chives. Serve with the dipping cup of ponzu.

notes   Using chopsticks will prevent the batter from becoming overworked; a loose batter that still has lumps of unmixed flour helps make a lighter, crisper batter. Ensure the water is very cold and prepare the batter just before cooking, as this will also help to make the finished results crisp.

If you can't find Mediterranean red shrimp, use tiger or Dublin Bay prawns. For the salad you can use any mixture of greens you prefer, but be sure you dress the salad only just before frying the shrimp.

Rock Shrimp Kakiage with Parmesan

Parmesan cheese adds another dimension of flavor to this wonderfully crisp *kakiage*—the Japanese term for a mixed tempura. Using a metal spatula or pancake turner helps stop the *kakiage* from breaking into pieces when it is first placed in the hot oil. When it has set as one piece, it can be gently removed from the utensil to continue cooking.

serves 2

vegetable oil, for deep-frying
1 green onion
4 ounces fresh rock shrimp or chopped tiger prawns
2 tablespoons sliced white onion
1/3 cup freshly grated Parmesan cheese
Tempura Batter (page 99)
chopped fresh parsley, for garnish
sea salt and freshly ground black pepper
1/4 lemon

1   Heat a medium-to-large pan of oil (3 1/4 to 4 inches deep) to a temperature of 350°F.

2   Chop the green onion into 1/4-inch pieces and place in a mixing bowl with the shrimp or prawns, onion, and all but 1 tablespoon of the grated Parmesan. Pour the tempura batter a little at a time into the mixing bowl so the contents are bound with the batter, but are slightly loose in the mixture. Divide the batter between 2 small cups or bowls.

3   Immerse a perfectly dry metal spatula or pancake turner horizontally into the hot oil so it is about 3/4 inch just below the surface. Pour the contents from the first cup carefully onto the spatula. As it begins to cook, slowly immerse it in the oil, so it stays in one piece. After 20 to 30 seconds, slide the mixture off the spatula with another metal spatula or something similar and cook for 3 to 4 minutes, turning it regularly until crisp and cooked through. Remove from the oil and drain on paper towels. Repeat the whole process with the contents of the second cup.

4   Place the cooked *kakiage* on a serving dish and sprinkle with the remaining Parmesan and the chopped parsley. Serve with the sea salt, black pepper, and a lemon quarter on the side. Eat while still hot and crisp.

Turbot Tempura

Slices of turbot are quickly fried in tempura batter to give a crisp texture on the outside while remaining deliciously soft on the inside, doing superb justice to the wonderfully flavored lean, firm flesh of the fish.

serves 4

4 ounces boneless, skinless fresh turbot fillet
vegetable oil, for deep-frying
tempura flour, for dusting
Tempura Batter (page 99)
1/2 red onion, thinly sliced
fresh cilantro leaves
a small quantity of Ama Zu Ponzu (page 249)

1   Place the turbot fillet on a chopping board with the skinned side up and the tail on the side of your preferred hand. Steadying the other end of the turbot with the fingers of your other hand, hold the knife in your preferred hand so the top is inclined sharply away from the fish. From the tail end of the fillet, start cutting fairly thick slices (1/4 inch), keeping the blade at that acute angle to achieve a clean cut across the grain.

2   Heat a medium-to-large pan of oil (3 1/4 to 4 inches deep) to a temperature of 350°F. Dust the slices of turbot in a little tempura flour and shake off any excess. Dip them into the cold tempura batter, allowing any excess batter to run off, then gently place in the hot oil, one at a time. Cook in 2 or 3 batches for 1 to 2 minutes each, until light and crisp. Remove with a slotted spoon and drain on paper towels.

3   Transfer the tempura fish to a serving dish, piling the pieces on top of one another, and scatter the sliced onion and a few cilantro leaves over. Pour the ponzu into the bottom of the plate and consume while still hot and crisp.

notes   This recipe is good for all firm white fish, such as sea bass, brill, sole, flounder, and lemon sole.

The cooked tempura should be eaten fairly soon after cooking, as the batter will soften due to the hot steam coming from the cooked fish flesh inside.

Caviar Tempura

This contrast of the crisp texture of the batter and the delicious saltiness of the caviar, finished with a squeeze of lemon juice, makes a truly mouth watering morsel. The first time you try this, it might be easiest to use monkfish, as it has a much firmer flesh and will be more forgiving.

5 ounces boneless, skinless fresh sea bass fillet
4 teaspoons Oscietra caviar
vegetable oil, for deep-frying
tempura flour, for dusting
Tempura Batter (page 99)
1 lemon, halved and thickly sliced

1   Place the sea bass fillet on a chopping board with the skinned side up and the tail on the side of your preferred hand. Steadying the other end of the sea bass with the fingers of the other hand, hold the knife in your preferred hand so the top is inclined sharply away from the fish. From the opposite end of the fillet, start cutting slices about 3/8 inch thick, keeping the blade at that acute angle so as to achieve slices with a width of about 1 inch. (You will need 8 good slices.)

2   With the tip of a small sharp knife, carefully cut a slit in one end of each slice of sea bass so it forms a pocket inside the slice; slowly work the knife tip in, to make the pocket as large as possible without creating any holes. Fill each pocket with about 1/2 teaspoon of caviar per slice, making sure the caviar is pushed well inside. (The handle of a teaspoon is good for this.) Secure the slit end of the slice with a toothpick, pushing it through and then back again so the caviar is sealed inside.

3   Heat a medium-to-large pan of oil (3 1/4 to 4 inches deep) to a temperature of 350°F. Carefully dust the stuffed sea bass slices in a little tempura flour and shake off any excess. Then, one at a time, dip them into the cold tempura batter, allow any excess batter to run off, and gently place them in the hot oil. Cook for 1 to 2 minutes, until the batter is light and crisp. Lift out with a slotted spoon and drain on paper towels.

4   To serve, place each slice on a serving spoon and serve with the lemon slices to squeeze over the top.

Whole Spiny Lobster Three Ways

Here spiny lobster is prepared in three different ways, as ceviche, sashimi, and tempura. A suitably grand way to serve a whole spiny lobster, it is well worth the end result. You can also make this dish with an ordinary lobster, using the blanched claws for the tempura part of the dish.

serves 4 to 6

1 live spiny lobster
1 lime

New-Style Spiny Lobster Ceviche
1/2 clove garlic, pureed
1 tablespoon finely shredded ginger
handful of chive stems
a little fresh aloe vera, thinly sliced
2 tablespoons Yuzu Soy (page 248)
2 tablespoons New-Style Oil (page 245)
pinch of white sesame seeds

Spiny Lobster with Sansho Pepper Salsa
1 teaspoon green sansho peppercorns (see page 252)
1 teaspoon seeded and finely chopped red chili
3 1/2 tablespoons finely chopped white onion
1 tablespoon olive oil
2 tablespoons fresh lemon juice
1/3 teaspoon salt

Spiny Lobster Tempura with Creamy Spicy Sauce
vegetable oil, for deep-frying
Tempura Batter (page 99)
small quantity of Creamy Spicy Sauce (page 246)
1 tablespoon snipped fresh chives

1 Put the lobster in the freezer for 20 minutes, so it goes into a deep sleep and won't be aware of the next stage.

2 Bring to a boil a saucepan of salted water large enough to cover the lobster. Plunge the lobster headfirst into the water for 1 minute. Remove the lobster and plunge it into a bowl of ice water to cool. This will enable the meat to be more easily removed from the shell.

3 Remove the tail from the body and carefully cut open the tail shell with a pair of scissors, then gently remove the tail meat. Starting at the thinner end, cut two-thirds of the tail meat into slices 1/16 inch thick, and then cut the remaining piece into 1/4-inch dice. If you like, you can reserve the lobster feelers and some shell for garnish.

4 To make the lobster ceviche, lay one-third of the lobster slices flat on a suitable serving dish. Dab the slices with a little garlic puree and sprinkle the ginger and chives evenly on top. Then add a few slices of aloe vera before spooning the soy over the top.

5 Heat a small pan with the oil until it just begins to smoke, then pour over the lobster slices to sear the tops. Finish by sprinkling with the sesame seeds.

6 To make the lobster with salsa, put the remaining tail meat slices in a suitable dish. Mix all the salsa ingredients together and spoon over the top.

7 To make the tempura, heat a medium-to-large pan of oil (3 3/4 to 4 inches deep) to a temperature of 350°F. Dip the diced lobster into the cold tempura batter, allowing any excess batter to run off, and then gently place in the hot oil. Cook for 1 to 2 minutes, until light and crisp, then remove and drain on paper towels. Place in a bowl and quickly mix with the spicy sauce while still hot. Serve sprinkled with the snipped chives.

8 Arrange the 3 separate dishes on a large serving platter and garnish with a lime cut in half, together with the lobster feelers and some shell, if you like.

Sea Urchin Tempura, London-Style

These delicate little parcels of sea urchin are actually wrapped in puff pastry dough and then quickly fried to encapsulate the full flavor of the sea.

serves 2

about 5 ounces puff pastry dough
2 fresh shiso leaves (see page 253)
1 teaspoon wasabi paste (see page 253)
3 1/2 ounces fresh sea urchin
vegetable oil, for deep-frying

garnish
sea salt
shichimi togarashi (see page 252)
1/2 lime

1   Roll out the puff pastry dough very thinly, no thicker than 1/16 inch. Using a round 2-inch pastry cutter, cut out 4 circles.

2   Place half a shiso leaf on each dough circle and spread a little of the wasabi in the middle of each. Divide the sea urchin evenly among the circles and close the dough around it, sealing at the top to form small purse shapes.

3   Heat a medium-to-large pan of oil (3 3/4 to 4 inches deep) to a temperature of 350°F and fry the purses for 1 to 2 minutes, until puffed and crisp on the outside.

4   Line a suitable dish with parchment paper and place the well-drained purses on it. Serve with sea salt, shichimi togarashi, and half of a lime on the side.

note   Take care when sealing the purses to make sure that there are no gaps where oil can get inside during cooking.

Sea Bass and Truffle Rolls

Here crisp egg rolls are filled with sea bass infused with the scented aroma of fresh white truffle.

serves 4

5 1/2 ounces boneless fresh sea bass fillet
2 large egg roll wrappers
1 egg, beaten
1/16 ounce white truffle, thinly sliced
sea salt and freshly ground black pepper
vegetable oil, for deep-frying
shichimi togarashi (see page 252)
a little karashi su-miso (see page 251)

1   Skin the sea bass fillet, reserving the skin for later. Cut the sea bass evenly into 4 pieces.

2   Working with 1 egg roll wrapper at a time, cut the sheet diagonally in half and place one piece on a flat surface with the point of the triangle away from you. Egg wash all the edges. Place a piece of sea bass and a few slices of the truffle in the middle of the edge nearest to you and season with salt and pepper. Fold first the left and then the right side of each wrapper into the middle over the sea bass, then roll the whole thing away from you, making sure the edges are completely sealed; repeat the process to make 3 more rolls. Take care that the rolls are completely sealed at the edges, otherwise the oil will get inside the roll during cooking.

3   Place a nonstick skillet over medium heat. Pressing it down with a metal spatula or pancake turner, cook the reserved sea bass skin in the dry pan, turning it occasionally until it becomes crisp.

4   Heat a medium-to-large pan of oil (3 3/4 to 4 inches deep) to a temperature of 350°F and fry the rolls in 2 batches in the hot oil for 3 to 4 minutes each batch, until golden brown. Lift them out with a slotted spoon and drain on paper towels.

5   Serve on a suitable dish, sprinkled with the remaining truffle slices. Place the crispy sea bass skin on top and serve more salt and black pepper, shichimi togarashi, and karashi su-miso separately.

Mackerel Nanban-Zuke

Here mackerel fillets are fried whole twice to get a really crisp exterior, then served with a sauce made from cider vinegar, soy sauce, and mirin to cut through the oiliness of the fish.

serves 2

sauce

pinch of shichimi togarashi (see page 252)

1 teaspoon sea salt

5 tablespoons apple cider vinegar

3 tablespoons mirin (see page 252)

3 tablespoons light soy sauce

1 cup Dashi (page 17)

3 tablespoons roughly chopped ginger

vegetable oil, for deep-frying

2 boneless fresh mackerel fillets, each about 3¹/₂ ounces

salt

arrowroot, for dusting

4 whole green onions, trimmed

4 fresh cilantro leaves on the stem

4 fresh flat-leaf parsley leaves on the stem

ito-togarashi (see page 251), for garnish

1   First make the sauce. Put all the ingredients together in a nonreactive saucepan and place over low heat. Bring to just below the boiling point, then strain and keep warm.

2   Heat a medium-to-large pan of oil (3³/₄ to 4 inches deep) to a temperature of 350°F. Season the mackerel fillets with salt and dust in the arrowroot, then fry in the hot oil for 2 to 3 minutes. Remove and let drain on paper towels. Repeat the process again, frying them for another 2 to 3 minutes, then drain.

3   Next, fry the whole green onions for 30 seconds. (Make sure that they are completely dry before placing them in the hot oil.) Remove and let drain.

4   Add the cilantro and parsley stems to the hot sauce for a few seconds to let them soften.

5   Place the mackerel fillets in a shallow bowl and pour a little of the sauce around them. Arrange the cilantro and parsley and the fried green onions on top of the fish. Garnish with the ito-togarashi and serve hot.

note   It is important that the sauce should not boil, otherwise it will become too intense in flavor.

Fish and Chips, Nobu-Style

Perfect party food—fish and chips all in one piece!

serves 6 to 8

2¹/4 pounds unpeeled russet or other good frying potatoes
2¹/4 pounds fresh cod, filleted and skinned
sea salt
3¹/2 tablespoons butter, softened
freshly ground black pepper
katakuriko (see page 251), for dusting
olive oil, for frying
malt vinegar, to serve

1 Start preparing this the day before you want to serve it. Steam the potatoes until half-cooked, about 10 minutes, then leave them to cool. When cool, peel them, then carefully cut them into slices little more than 1/2 inch thick.

2 Season the cod with a little salt and place in a colander for about 15 minutes to let some of the excess water from the fish drain away, then rinse under cold running water and pat completely dry.

3 Heat the oven to 325°F. Brush the inside of a 9-inch terrine with the soft butter, then line it with plastic wrap, making sure you have plenty of plastic wrap overhanging the edges to cover the top of the filling.

4 Cut the potato slices to the same width as the terrine and place them in the bottom, making sure it is completely covered; season with salt and pepper. Trim the cod fillet to the same shape as the terrine, making sure it is slightly more than 1/2 inch thick (you will need 2 pieces like this) and lay on top of the potato. Repeat the potato and cod layers and finish with a third layer of potato. Wrap the plastic wrap over the top to seal everything, then put the lid on the terrine.

5 Place the terrine in a deep roasting pan filled with boiling water, then put that in the oven and cook for 30 minutes. Test to see if the terrine is cooked by placing a metal skewer into the middle. If it is easily pierced and the tip of the skewer is hot when withdrawn, it is ready.

6 Remove the lid and leave the terrine to cool for 20 minutes, then place some weights on the top to press the terrine. (Cans of beans, or tomatoes, are good for this.) Place in the refrigerator for a minimum of 24 hours to set completely.

7 Next day, dip the terrine briefly into warm water, then carefully turn it out onto a clean board and remove all the plastic wrap. With a sharp knife, carefully cut the terrine into thick slices (about 3/4 inch). Then cut these into fat "chip" shapes.

8 Dust the slices in katakuriko and fry in some olive oil in a nonstick pan until crisp and brown; remove and drain on paper towels.

9 Serve these "chips" on pieces of paper with sea salt and vinegar on the side.

note For the terrine to be firm enough to slice properly, it must be pressed well, so don't be frightened to put too much weight on it. The heavier the weight, the better the pressing.

Savoy Cabbage Steak Salad

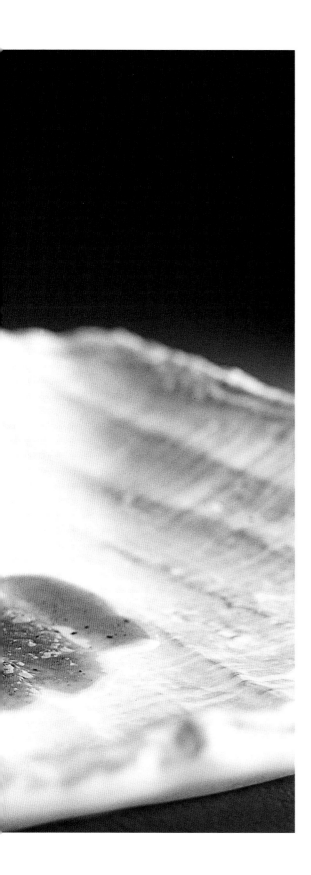

When cooking this dish, the sugars in the cabbage caramelize, giving it a wonderful flavor. It's even better when it's accompanied with the Matsuhisa Dressing. We like to call these cabbage rolls "steaks," like slices of fish.

serves 4

1 large head of savoy cabbage
olive oil, for cooking
sea salt
1 clove garlic, thinly sliced
Matsuhisa Dressing (page 242)
2 tablespoons shredded daikon (see page 250)

1 Cut off and discard the stem end of the cabbage, then separate the leaves. Blanch these quickly in boiling salted water for 20 seconds; refresh in ice water and drain well.

2 Spread out a sheet of foil about 18 by 8 inches. Pile the cabbage leaves on the foil on top of one another, starting with the largest first and alternating the direction of the leaves so they lie flat and maintain an even thickness. When assembled, the leaves should look balanced. Roll them up in the foil, from the edge, firmly pressing down as you roll. The roll should form a cylinder about 4 inches in diameter. Secure the foil around the rolled cabbage with string at intervals about 2 inches apart. Cut the foil-wrapped roll in between the strings into cylinders about 2 inches long.

3 Heat a skillet with some olive oil in it and season the open ends of the cabbage with a generous amount of sea salt. Fry them, one open end down, adding the sliced garlic to flavor the oil. Turn them over after 3 to 4 minutes and cook the other sides. The cabbage rolls are ready when both ends are lightly caramelized.

4 Cut the string and remove the foil. Pile the cylinders on a serving plate, cooked sides upward, and dress with the dressing and a little shredded daikon.

bake

Wood-Roasted Vegetables

Wood-roasted baby vegetables are combined with yuzu juice and miso to accentuate their smoky flavor. We have a new wood-fired oven in Nobu Berkeley Street and this is one of the dishes devised especially for it. If you don't have access to one, you can use a conventional oven or grill the vegetables on a charcoal barbecue first, before placing them in a conventional oven, to create the smoky effect.

serves 2

1 small bunch of thin yellow green beans, blanched

4 slices of sweet potato

4 broccoli florets

2 shiitake mushrooms

2 cep (porcini) mushrooms

1/2 bunch of enoki mushrooms

4 baby corn cobs

2 baby zucchini

4 baby tomatoes

1/2 head of Belgian endive, cut into quarters lengthwise

2 slices of lotus root (see page 251)

1 clove garlic, thinly sliced

a little olive oil

sea salt and freshly ground black pepper

1/4 cup Yuzu Miso Sauce (page 78)

1 Heat a wood-fired or pizza oven to 400°F. Trim any vegetables that are large, so everything is roughly the same size. Place in a bowl and mix in the garlic slices. Lightly dress with a little olive oil and season with salt and pepper.

2 Arrange the coated vegetables neatly in a shallow ovenproof casserole or earthenware dish and bake in the oven for 10 minutes.

3 Drizzle the sauce over the top and serve in the cooking dish.

note You can use any variety of vegetables or mushrooms for this dish as long as they have similar cooking times. If using any large root vegetables, they must first be blanched and cut into suitable sizes.

Baked Eggplant with Bonito and Dashi Ponzu

In this elegantly simple dish, the smoky flavors of roasted eggplant and the bonito flakes are enhanced with ginger-flavored soy sauce and rice vinegar.

serves 4

1 long eggplant
small handful of bonito flakes (see page 250)
5 tablespoons Dashi Ponzu (page 244)
1 tablespoon grated ginger

1   Heat the oven to 450°F. Cut the eggplant in half and then into quarters lengthwise and place on a metal baking sheet or similar. Roast in the oven for 5 minutes, or until the skin is brown and the flesh is soft.

2   Place the baked eggplant on a chopping board and, while it is still hot, cut into bite-size pieces. Transfer to a suitable serving dish, shaping it to look like the original eggplant again.

3   Sprinkle the bonito flakes over the top. Pour the ponzu into a dipping cup and place this on the dish, together with a small mound of grated ginger.

4   To eat, mix a little of the grated ginger into the ponzu and then dip the pieces of eggplant into the sauce.

note   When the eggplant is hot and you sprinkle the bonito flakes on top, the rising heat from the eggplant makes the bonito flakes move and dance as if they were in the wind.

Baked Mushrooms

This is a great way to enjoy all types of mushroom, baked and flavored with sake, olive oil, and yuzu juice. You can vary the types of mushroom used in this dish to suit your taste or availability.

serves 4

1³/4 ounces morels

1³/4 ounces button mushrooms

1³/4 ounces eringe mushrooms (see page 250)

1³/4 ounces cep (porcini) mushrooms

2 tablespoons olive oil

2 cloves garlic, sliced

2 tablespoons sake

sea salt and freshly ground black pepper

1 tablespoon yuzu juice (see page 253) or fresh lemon juice

1/2 red chili, seeded and thinly sliced

1   Heat the oven to 450°F. Wipe and clean the mushrooms. (The morels might need to be soaked to remove any sand or stiffly brushed, see note below.) Cut any larger ones into evenly sized pieces, but try to keep the mushrooms whole if possible.

2   Place the mushrooms, olive oil, garlic, and sake in an ovenproof earthenware pot or casserole dish with a tight-fitting lid. Season with sea salt and pepper and mix well to ensure all the mushrooms are coated; cover tightly.

3   Bake in the oven for 12 minutes.

4   Remove the lid, add the yuzu juice, and mix in. Sprinkle with the sliced chili and serve.

note   Because of their pitted surface, a good way of cleaning morels without soaking them is to use a small stiff brush, like a nailbrush.

Baked Cabbage with White Truffle

This dish is a new addition to the menu in one of our London restaurants and has been an instant success. The outer cabbage leaves become slightly sweet when they brown in the oven and the addition of truffles makes this a real earthy dish.

serves 4 to 6

1 head of pointed (summer) cabbage
¹/4 cup sake
¹/4 cup clarified butter (see note, right)
sea salt and freshly ground black pepper
shichimi togarashi (see page 252)
1 white truffle

1   Heat the oven to 450°F. Peel off the tough outer leaves from the cabbage and discard. Wash the remaining cabbage and drain. Cut the cabbage in half lengthwise and then cut each half lengthwise into 3 equal segments.

2   Place the cabbage wedges on a shallow baking tray or dish and pour the sake and the clarified butter over. Season with sea salt and black pepper, and cover the tray tightly with foil.

3   Bake in the oven for 8 minutes, then remove the tray, take off the foil, and return the tray to the oven. Bake for 3 to 4 minutes longer, so the outside cabbage leaves begin to brown and caramelize.

4   Remove the cabbage wedges from the tray with a metal spatula and place on a suitable serving dish. Spoon the juices from the tray over the cabbage, sprinkle a little shichimi togarashi on top, and slice the white truffle over the top.

notes   You can use dried red chili instead of the shichimi and replace the white truffle with black truffle or even just a few drops of truffle oil—it even tastes great just on its own. In the restaurant, we do this in a wood-fired oven, but a conventional oven is perfectly adequate.

To clarify butter, heat it very slowly in a small pan and skim off the foam that gathers on the top. After a minute or so, very gently pour off the clear liquid, leaving any milk solids behind. The butter can now be heated without burning so readily.

Salt-Baked Abalone

Baking abalone in a salt crust retains and enhances the full, natural flavors of the sea in them. The blanched cabbage leaves really just serve to hold the salt crust in place around the abalone.

serves 2

2 fresh abalone
2 large cabbage leaves
1 cup fine salt
white of 1 egg
small quantity of Yuzu Miso Sauce (page 78)
1/2 lemon, halved and cut into thick slices

1   Heat the oven to 400°F. Extract the abalone from its shell and remove any dirt or debris. Cut away the hard, projecting black sections around the edge, then rinse under cold water. Scrub the abalone shells to remove any debris inside and out, then boil the shells in salted water for 10 minutes.

2   Blanch the cabbage leaves in another pan of salted, boiling water for 30 seconds and drain.

3   Place the 1 cup salt in a mixing bowl, then mix in just enough egg white to moisten it and create a fairly dry paste.

4   Cover each abalone completely with the salt mixture and wrap each one in a cabbage leaf to help hold the salt in place.

5   Bake in the oven for 30 minutes, then remove. Leave to cool for 5 minutes before taking off the cabbage leaves and the salt crust.

6   Cut each abalone into slices 1/4 inch thick and dress back in their shells. Place on a dish, spoon a little miso over each, and serve with the lemon slices.

note   Use small to medium abalone for this dish.

Baby Squid with Ginger Salsa

Here a quick blast in a very hot oven with baby vegetables and ginger gives a new dimension of flavor to baby squid. They require only the briefest of baking to be perfectly cooked.

serves 2

8 baby zucchini
olive oil, for brushing
6 or 7 baby tomatoes
3¹/2 ounces cleaned fresh baby squid
sea salt and freshly ground black pepper
¹/4 cup Ginger Salsa (page 243)

1   Heat a broiler or barbecue. Lightly brush the zucchini with olive oil and broil or barbecue for 2 minutes, turning them halfway; leave to cool.

2   Heat the oven to 450°F. Place the tomatoes, squid, and zucchini in a bowl and season with sea salt and pepper and a little olive oil. Put all the ingredients in an ovenproof ceramic dish or similar and spoon the salsa over the top.

3   Bake for 5 minutes and serve straight from the oven.

note   Try to pick even-size squid so they cook in the same time; if some are much larger than the rest, cut them into smaller pieces.

Razor Clams Cooked with Celery, Cucumber, and Olive oil

Here the clams are simply baked, shelled, and tossed with a crunchy cucumber, olive, and celery salad, lifted with an olive oil and sake and soy sauce dressing. The dish is delightfully finished with the rich flavor and extra textural delight of a sprinkling of mouth-popping salmon eggs.

serves 2

6 fresh razor clams
2 tablespoons diced celery
2 tablespoons diced cucumber
1 tablespoon diced pitted green olives
2 tablespoons salmon eggs

dressing
3 tablespoons olive oil
1/2 teaspoon sea salt
2 tablespoons Sake Soy (page 248)
1 teaspoon freshly ground black pepper

1   Heat the oven to 400°F. Rinse the clams well under cold running water to remove any sand and place on a metal baking sheet.

2   Mix the celery, cucumber, and olives together in a bowl.

3   In another bowl, combine the dressing ingredients.

4   Roast the clams in the oven for 5 minutes, then remove and let cool.

5   When they are cool enough to handle, remove the meat from the shells, discarding any clams that have not opened. On a chopping board, remove the tip of the siphon, the gills, and the digestive tract (the dark parts of the clam) with a knife and discard. Cut the flesh roughly into 1 1/4 inch pieces and add to the bowl of celery, cucumber, and olives. Toss together with the dressing.

6   Spoon onto a serving dish and sprinkle the salmon eggs on top to serve.

note   Make sure the razor clams are live when they go into the oven, and discard any that fail to open when you take them out.

Frothing Crab

Here steamed crabmeat is returned to its shell and dressed with sea urchin and Parmesan cheese, then covered in egg white and fried. The egg white froths and resembles the bubbles that come from a live crab. This technique is called *koura-age* by the Japanese.

serves 2

1 large live (or freshly cooked) crab
2 tablespoons masago (smelt roe, see page 251)
sea salt and freshly ground black pepper
1 3/4 ounces fresh sea urchin, chopped
1 3/4 ounces cep (porcini) mushrooms, sliced
2 tablespoons chopped green onion
2 tablespoons grated Parmesan cheese
whites of 2 eggs
vegetable oil, for deep-frying
edible seaweed, for garnish

1   If the crab is live, steam or boil it for 20 minutes over high heat. Remove from the water or steamer and let drain and cool. When it is cool enough to handle, remove the legs and claws from the body, then crack the claws and the legs and remove all the white meat, putting it into a bowl. Be careful not to leave any small bits of shell in the meat.

2   Place the shell body on its back and remove the central body part (the piece where the legs were attached) from the shell. Using a chopstick, remove any white meat from the leg joints and add to the claw and leg crabmeat. With a spoon, scoop out the soft brown meat only and add to the bowl, then remove all remaining parts from inside the shell and discard. Rinse out the shell with water and drain.

3   Add the smelt roe to the crabmeat and season with salt and pepper. Add a layer of the mixed crabmeat to the shell, covering the whole cavity inside, and then put a layer of sea urchin on top. Cover the sea urchin with a layer of mushrooms, then the green onion, and finally the Parmesan cheese.

4   Beat the egg whites in a clean bowl until they form stiff peaks, then cover all the filling inside the crab shell with the beaten egg white and smooth over the top with a metal spatula.

5   Bring about 1 3/4 inches of oil in a shallow pan to 325°F. Slip the shell carefully into the oil, egged side up, and cook for 10 minutes, until the beaten egg white puffs up. Carefully remove and place on a suitable serving dish.

6   Dress with the seaweed and serve immediately.

notes   During cooking, make sure the height of the oil is no more than the height of the shell. The oil should not be so high that it gets inside the shell from the top.
  By the time the egg white begins to froth and cook, the crab filling inside will be thoroughly heated through.

Roasted Toro Collar Steak

Rich and juicy toro (tuna) collar is roasted quickly in the oven and then simply served with a spicy lemon, soy, and vinegar sauce to cut through the oiliness of the tuna flesh.

serves 2

1 tablespoon grated daikon (see page 250)
1 teaspoon red chili paste
2 tuna collar steaks, each about 5 ounces
olive oil, for brushing
sea salt and freshly ground black pepper
1 tablespoon shredded green onion
1 tablespoon grated green mooli
Ponzu (page 248)
2 pickled ginger stems (hajikami, see page 251)

1   Heat the oven to 400°F.

2   Mix together the daikon and the red chili paste in a small bowl and set aside.

3   Brush the tuna steaks with olive oil, season with salt and pepper, and place on a flat metal roasting tray.

4   Cook in the oven for 8 to 10 minutes, depending on the thickness of the steaks.

5   Transfer to a serving dish and place the daikon and chili mixture, the green onion, and the green mooli in 3 neat little piles on the dish, along with a dipping bowl of the ponzu. Serve while still hot, garnished with the ginger stems.

notes   The tuna collar steaks are cut from the head and have a high fat content, rather like that of tuna belly, which is actually best suited to this dish.

When eating this, place a little of the chili mix, green onion, and green mooli into the dipping sauce with it.

Crispy-Skin Poussin

The baby chicken is cooked quickly in a hot oven to crisp the skin nicely and it is then drenched in Spicy Lemon Dressing. It can also be cooked without the cabbage stuffing, in which case it should then be cooked flat on a baking tray and the cooking time reduced by about 5 minutes.

serves 2

1 whole poussin (baby chicken)
1/4 head of pointed (summer) cabbage, finely shredded
olive oil, for brushing
sea salt and freshly ground black pepper
1 head of Belgian endive, split in half lengthwise
3 cherry tomatoes
3 tablespoons Spicy Lemon Dressing (page 242)
1/4 lemon

1   Heat the oven to 400°F.

2   Place the poussin, breast side down, on a chopping board and cut through the skin down to the bone in the middle of its back. Making small cuts, remove the meat away from each side of the carcass. Cut the wing and leg joints at the knuckle and separate from the carcass, then remove the wishbone and continue cutting away the breasts from the breastbone to leave the carcass completely separate from the breasts and legs. Bone out the thigh bones from the legs, keeping the leg and breast meat still attached together in one whole piece.

3   Season the inside of the bird and the shredded cabbage with salt and pepper. Place the cabbage in the middle of the bird and wrap the sides of the bird around the cabbage so they overlap. Place on a baking tray, then brush lightly with olive oil and season.

4   Cut the Belgian endive into quarters lengthwise and brush them and the whole cherry tomatoes with olive oil; season.

5   Cook the poussin in the oven for 15 minutes, then add the cherry tomatoes and Belgian endive to the baking tray and roast for 10 minutes longer.

6   Place the poussin on a suitable serving dish and garnish with the Belgian endive and cherry tomatoes. Spoon the lemon-flavored dressing over and garnish with lemon wedges.

steam

Razor Clams Three Ways

Here we cook razor clams in three different ways and serve them alongside one another. The contrasts of different textures and flavors this provides make for a very exciting dish.

In case any clams turn out to be dead and so don't open when cooked, it is a good idea to buy one or two extra.

serves 2

6 fresh razor clams

Creamy Spicy Clams
2 teaspoons masago (smelt roe, see page 251)
2 teaspoons finely shredded green onion
small quantity of Creamy Spicy Sauce (page 246)

Black Bean Sauce Clams
1 tablespoon sake
2 teaspoons Spicy Black Bean Sauce (page 246)
1 tablespoon finely shredded ginger

New-Style Clams
1 tablespoon Sake Soy (page 248)
1 teaspoon garlic puree
1 tablespoon finely shredded ginger
1 tablespoon fresh chive strips
2 tablespoons New-Style Oil (page 245)

1   Soak the clams overnight in plenty of cold water with a little salt; this helps remove any sand from their digestive tracts.

2   Bring a pan of salted water to a boil and put in the clams for 30 seconds, then remove and refresh under cold running water. Discard any that have not opened.

3   Remove the clam meat from the shells and cut away the stomach (this is the dark part), then cut each one at an angle into 3 or 4 pieces. Arrange the pieces in the 6 best-looking half-shells and discard the rest.

4   For the Creamy Spicy Clams, heat a broiler and broil 2 of the filled half-shells for 3 minutes until cooked. Spread with the masago and green onion and cover with the spicy sauce, then broil again until the sauce just begins to brown.

5   For the Black Bean Sauce Clams, prepare a steamer or pan with a tight-fitting lid and a little water in the bottom. Have a plate on hand to hold the clams out of the water. Take 2 more filled half-shells, pour the sake over them, and spread a teaspoon of black bean sauce on each one, followed by a little shredded ginger; steam them for 3 minutes.

6   For the New-Style Clams, take the remaining 2 filled half-shells, pour the sake-flavored soy over, and steam them for 3 minutes. When cooked, rub the clam meat with the garlic puree and place the ginger and chives on top. Heat the oil in a small pan until it just begins to smoke, and immediately pour over the top of the clams.

7   To serve, arrange the 3 different types of clam alternating on a suitable serving dish.

note   You can, of course, try just one of the cooking methods at a time if you prefer. Any of the three cooking methods works well with mussels as well as clams.

Steamed Clams with Ginger and Garlic

This simple dish of steamed clams is flavored with ginger, garlic, and toasted sesame oil, and produces a wonderful aromatic broth.

serves 4

2¹/4 pounds fresh cherrystone clams

2 cloves garlic, sliced

1-inch piece of ginger, peeled and cut into thin strips

1 tablespoon grapeseed oil

1¹/2 teaspoons toasted sesame oil

1 leek, white part only, cut lengthwise into long strips

1 cup Dashi (page 17)

soy sauce

freshly ground black pepper

1   Wash the clams thoroughly and place in a saucepan with the rest of the ingredients, except the soy sauce and pepper. Cover with a lid and cook over high heat for 10 minutes, or until the clams have opened.

2   Transfer the clams to a suitable dish, discarding any that have stayed closed. Add soy sauce and pepper to taste to the cooking liquid and then pour this over the top of the clams.

note   You can also use this method with mussels, and both make great dressings for noodles and pasta.

Slow-Cooked Salmon

Making this dish requires a little patience, but the rewards are certainly well worth it. This sort of slow cooking produces salmon that looks almost raw, but does give it a very soft and delicate texture—and in the process also creates its own flavorsome cooking juices. To cook this dish in this way, you will need a

kitchen thermometer, to help keep the cooking temperature steady, and a plastic boiling bag to gain the best results.

2 fresh salmon fillets, each about 3 1/2 ounces, skinned and boned
1 tablespoon sake
1 tablespoon light soy sauce
1 tablespoon Dashi (page 17)
1/2-inch piece of ginger, peeled and finely shredded
2 tablespoons butter
1 clove garlic, sliced

garnish
1 1/3 cups snow peas, shredded
olive oil, for sautéing
salt and freshly ground black pepper
fresh shiso leaves (see page 253)

1   Bring a pan of water up to 149°F and maintain the temperature with the aid of a thermometer.

2   Place all the ingredients, except the garnish items, in a boiling bag. Immerse the bag in the water and, checking with the thermometer, maintain a temperature of 149°F for 12 minutes. Regulate the temperature by removing the pan from the heat if it becomes too hot and vice versa. Make sure no water enters the bag; it must remain completely waterproof.

3   Meanwhile, sauté the snow peas for the garnish quickly in a little olive oil and season with salt and pepper, then arrange in the middle of a plate.

4   Remove the salmon carefully from the bag (it might be easier to pour it into a small dish first) and slice gently or leave whole if preferred, then place on top of the snow peas. Spoon a little of the juices from the bag around the salmon and garnish with shiso cress.

note   It is important that the temperature remains at a constant 149°F during the cooking process to gain the maximum effect of the slow cooking.

Steamed Scorpion Fish

Steaming helps keep the purity and juiciness of the scorpion fish, while the ginger, garlic, and sesame add a wonderful aroma to the flesh.

serves 4 to 6

2¹/4 pounds whole fresh scorpion fish, cleaned, scaled, and dressed
2 cloves garlic, thinly sliced
2 tablespoons finely shredded ginger
4 cep (porcini) mushrooms, cut in half
4 eringe mushrooms (see page 250), cut in half
2 tablespoons sake
¹/2 bunch of chives, finely snipped
3 tablespoons New-Style Oil (page 245)
3 tablespoons Sake Soy (page 248)
small handful of thin green beans, blanched
1 summer truffle, thinly sliced
steamed rice, to serve

1   Rinse the fish inside and out with cold water, pat dry with paper towels, and place on a chopping board. On each side of the fish, make parallel angled cuts about ³/4 inch apart just through to the bone. This enables the heat to penetrate and cook the fish evenly.

2   Place the fish on a heatproof serving plate and spread the garlic and ginger across the length of the tail, then arrange the ceps and eringe mushrooms down one side. Pour the sake over and steam in a steamer for 12 to 15 minutes, until cooked—check with a knife at the thickest part to see if it is done.

3   When the fish is ready, sprinkle the chives over the tail and heat the oil until just smoking. Pour the soy over the fish and add the green beans and truffle slices. Finish by pouring the hot oil over the ginger, chives, and garlic slices on the tail to sear and release the flavors.

4   Serve with bowls of steamed rice.

note   For more than 4 people use more than one fish. Each fish should not be any heavier than 2¹/4 pounds, unless you have a very large steamer. Ask your fish merchant to clean and scale the fish, leaving the head and fins intact. You can tell if the fish is fresh by the clearness of the eyes, the springiness of the flesh, and the bright red color of the gills.

Steamed John Dory with Wild Garlic Leaves en Papillote

When John Dory is filleted, each of the two fillets naturally splits into three pieces, which, when folded in half, make perfect parcels for steaming. John Dory develops a beautifully silken texture when steamed, and the wild garlic leaves add a wonderful aroma that will surprise your guests when the packages are opened at the table.

serves 6

1 large fresh John Dory, skinned and filleted, then each fillet
  separated into 3 pieces (see above)
6 shiitake mushrooms, wiped and stems removed
4 ounces oyster mushrooms, wiped and stems removed (about
  1²/3 cups)
12 asparagus spears, each cut at an angle into 3 pieces,
  then briefly blanched
3 ounces wild garlic leaves (ramsons or bear garlic), coarsely
  chopped
4 tablespoons butter
sea salt and freshly ground black pepper
shichimi togarashi (see page 252)
6 tablespoons sake
6 tablespoons soy sauce

1 You will need a steamer big enough to cook the 6 packages together. Preheat the oven to 300°F. Cut out six 16-inch-diameter circles from parchment paper. Or do what we do in the restaurant kitchens, which is to take a piece of parchment bigger than the circle needed and fold it in half, then in half again at right angles to the first fold, and repeat this 3 times. Trim the open end of the folded parchment to the length of the radius of the required circle (8 inches). When you open the paper out, it will be an almost perfect circle.

2 Place a folded piece of fish neatly in the middle of each of the parchment circles. Scatter one-sixth of the mushrooms, asparagus, and wild garlic leaves over each of the pieces of fish. Then place 2 teaspoons of butter on top of each and season with salt, pepper, and shichimi togarashi.

3 Fold each of the parchment circles into a half-moon shape, taking care that the contents remain in the middle of the bag. Fold one of the corners up so it is at right angles to the flat side of the half-moon. Now fold the rounded edge of the parcel over with tight little folds, each one overlapping the next until you are two-thirds of the way around. Holding the last fold tightly, pick up the bag (making sure the sealed end is pointing downward) and pour 1 tablespoon each of the sake and soy sauce into the opening. Fold up the last corner, again at right angles to the bottom, and continue making tight little folds around the top until you reach the end. Tuck the end around into the last corner and stand the package on its flat end. (It should look like a pastry.)

4 Place the packages in the steamer and steam for 10 to 12 minutes, then remove them carefully and place them on a baking tray. Put in the heated oven for 1 minute to dry the paper and let the bags puff up a little. Take care that the parchment doesn't burn while in the oven.

5 Serve immediately, cutting open the top of each package at the table.

notes You can use this treatment with any fish, adjusting the cooking time according to the thickness of the fish. If wild garlic is not available, try spinach or celery leaves. For a really special treat, add a few truffle shavings to each package.

Spring Vegetable Medleys

This is the best way to appreciate these baby vegetables, as they are lightly steamed to retain a slight crunch and then tossed in a selection of appropriate dressings.

serves 4

1 small bunch of thin green beans
1 small bunch of thin yellow beans
4 baby carrots
4 baby turnips
4 baby beets
1/4 small pumpkin squash
4 red radishes
1 ripe fig, quartered
Matsuhisa Dressing (page 242)
Jalapeño Dressing (page 242)
Spicy Lemon Dressing (page 242)

1   Trim the beans, carrots, turnips, and beets, then trim and remove any seeds from the pumpkin.

2   Steam the vegetables separately: the cooking times will vary depending on their size and type. The beans will cook quickly, as will the pumpkin, then the carrots next, and finally the turnips and beets should take the longest. Check after 3 minutes to see how they are progressing, remembering you need them to be slightly al dente.

3   When they are cooked, place them in bowls with the radishes and fig quarters, and dress with the sauces. Alternatively, place the vegetables together and keep the sauces separate, so your guests can choose their favorite to go with each different vegetable.

note   Try experimenting with different types of baby vegetables.

sauté

King Crab with Onion-Ginger Salsa

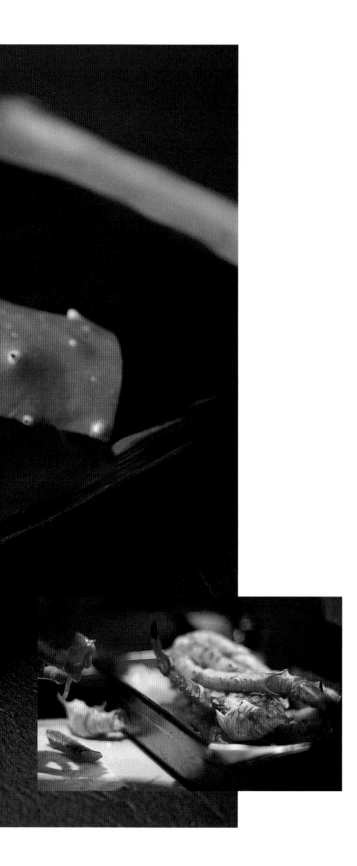

Here, king crab is quickly sautéed to retain its natural juices, then enhanced with Ginger Salsa. King crab legs are usually sold already cooked.

serves 2

2 cooked king crab legs
sea salt and freshly ground black pepper
1 tablespoon clarified butter (see page 126)
1 tablespoon plus 1 teaspoon sake
small handful of daikon radish sprouts (kaiware, see page 251)
1/4 cup Ginger Salsa (page 243)

1   With a pair of scissors, cut away the shell around the crab legs (keeping the nicest pieces for decoration), leaving the meat in one piece. Remove any sinews from the end of the meat with a pair of tweezers or small pliers.

2   Heat a skillet over medium heat and season the crab legs with salt and pepper. Add the clarified butter to the pan and quickly sauté the crab legs for 1 to 2 minutes on all sides.

3   Add the sake and allow almost all of it to evaporate, then add the daikon sprouts and leave to cook for 3 seconds only. Remove from the pan, together with the crabmeat.

4   Place the crab legs on a suitable serving dish with the daikon sprouts alongside. Spoon the salsa over the crab legs and garnish with the pieces of crab shell.

note   Eating crabmeat actually lowers the body's temperature and the ginger brings it back up, to balance out the effect. You can make this dish with cooked legs from ordinary crabs.

Baby Octopus Toban

The toban is a ceramic dish with a lid in which the food is cooked from the heat in the bottom and is then served sizzling at the table. The aromas that are released when the lid is removed are a wondrous delight. In this recipe, the flavor of the baby octopus is heightened with the saltiness of dried miso and the heat of the shichimi.

serves 2

12 to 16 (7 ounces) fresh baby octopus
1 tablespoon olive oil
2 tablespoons clarified butter (see page 126)
1 clove garlic, thinly sliced
8 okra, blanched
1/4 cup sake
2 tablespoons yuzu juice (see page 253)
shichimi togarashi (see page 252)
2 teaspoons Dried Miso (page 249)

1   Cut out and remove the beak from each octopus, then push out the eyes from behind and cut them off. Turn the head inside out, remove all the innards, and rinse thoroughly in running cold water. Rub the octopus in a bowl with salt to remove the slime, then rinse under cold water.

2   Heat a broiler and lightly broil the octopus on all sides for 1 minute.

3   Place two toban dish bottoms over medium heat and allow to heat through. Working quickly, so the octopus isn't overcooked, divide the olive oil and the clarified butter between the toban dishes, followed by the sliced garlic, octopus, and okra. Let cook for a few seconds.

4   Pour in the sake, followed by the yuzu juice, then finish with a pinch of shichimi on top of each and the miso.

5   Place the lids on and serve while still sizzling.

note   When bringing this dish to the table, make sure you sit it on a heatproof mat or another heatproof dish, as the heat from the ceramic bottom can scorch the table. When removing the lid from a toban at the table, always use a heatproof cloth to prevent scalding.

Dover Sole with Spicy Shiso Ponzu

Dover sole is always a favorite in our London restaurants, and its delicate but firm flesh is perfectly matched by this tangy dressing.

serves 2

vegetable oil, for deep-frying

1 fresh Dover sole, about 14 ounces, filleted and skinned (but backbone reserved and head removed)

sea salt and freshly ground black pepper

flour, for dusting

2 tablespoons olive oil

1 tablespoon clarified butter (see page 126)

1/4 cup Shiso Ponzu (page 244)

whole shiitake mushrooms, for garnish

1   Heat a medium-to-large pan of oil (3³/₄ to 4 inches deep) to a temperature of 350°F. Using a pair of chopsticks, hold the tail of the sole bone and carefully lower it into the hot oil. Let it cook for 2 to 3 minutes, until it is completely crisp. Again using chopsticks, remove it from the oil, place one end on a clean, flat surface, and bend the bone into a "U" shape (this will be possible only while it is still hot); let drain on paper towels.

2   Season the sole fillets with salt and pepper, and lightly dust in flour, shaking off any excess. Heat a large nonstick skillet over medium heat and add the olive oil and clarified butter. Place the fillets in the pan, skin side down, and gently sauté for 2 minutes; then turn them over and cook for 1 to 2 minutes longer.

3   Carefully remove from the pan and place the fillets side by side on a serving dish. Spoon the ponzu around them and place the fried bone over the top. Garnish with some shiitake mushrooms.

note   The crisp, fried bone can be eaten as well. Lemon sole and flounder are good substitutes if Dover sole is not available.

Monkfish with Fennel Salad

Monkfish and fennel is a classic combination in Western cooking, but here we have given it a Japanese twist, with the addition of a tangy hot-and-sour dressing.

serves 2

5 baby fennel bulbs
sea salt and freshly ground black pepper
2 tablespoons fresh orange juice
2 tablespoons olive oil, plus more for cooking
5 ounces boneless, skinless fresh monkfish fillet
flour, for dusting
6 baby plum tomatoes
small quantity of Spicy Sour Sauce (page 246)

1 Thinly slice the baby fennel on a mandoline grater and place the slices in a nonreactive bowl. Season with salt and pepper, add the orange juice and olive oil, and toss well.

2 Slice the monkfish across into medallions about $1/2$ inch thick. Pat these dry with paper towels, then season with salt and pepper.

3 Heat some olive oil in a nonstick skillet over high heat. Dust the monkfish with flour and shake off any excess. Cook the fish medallions for 2 minutes on each side and drain on a metal rack.

4 Drain off any excess liquid from the baby fennel and place a neat pile on a serving dish. Arrange the monkfish around the fennel and decorate with the baby plum tomatoes and a little sauce.

note Monkfish has a high water content, so the flour helps to form a seal around the flesh during cooking.

Crispy Gloucester Old Spot Pork Belly with Spicy Miso

Succulent, crisp pork belly is here combined with ginger, garlic, and Spicy Miso—and its hint of toasted sesame oil. Gloucester Old Spot is a traditional rare breed of pig from the apple orchards of Gloucestershire, England, distinguished by its large, floppy ears and black spots on its back, as well as the succulence and fine full flavor of its meat. Ancient folklore claims that the spots are bruises caused by apples falling on the pigs as they foraged in the orchards for food.

serves 4

18 ounces Gloucester Old Spot pork belly, bones removed
2 red chilies, split in half lengthwise
3 1/2 ounces ginger, peeled and sliced
4 cloves garlic, sliced
sea salt and freshly ground black pepper

garnish
6 tablespoons Spicy Miso (page 245)
1 tablespoon finely diced seeded red chili
1 tablespoon finely snipped fresh chives or green onion
1 tablespoon finely diced red onion

1 Using a very sharp knife, carefully remove the skin from the pork belly, keeping as much fat as possible attached to the belly meat.

2 Place the belly in a flat, shallow heavy-based pan just large enough for it to sit snugly on the bottom. Add the chilies, ginger, and garlic, and season with salt and pepper. Add just enough water to cover the belly and place a plate on top to keep the belly submersed in the liquid, then cover with the lid.

3 Place over high heat and bring to a boil, then reduce the heat to a bare simmer and simmer for 1 hour. (Check from time to time that the pork belly is always immersed in the stock, and top off with more water if necessary.) Remove from the heat and leave the belly to cool in the stock, then refrigerate overnight.

4 Remove the pork belly from the stock, drain, and pat dry with paper towels. Cut it into strips about 3/4 inch wide.

5 Place a dry nonstick skillet over high heat and fry the pork belly strips on all sides until uniformly golden brown and crisp, adjusting the heat where necessary during cooking; drain on paper towels.

6 While the meat is still hot, place the strips on a clean chopping board and cut into bite-size cubes.

7 Spoon half the miso sauce onto the bottom of a suitable serving dish and arrange the pork belly pieces on top. Spoon the remaining sauce over the top of the pork. Mix the finely chopped chili, chives, and red onion together and sprinkle on the top of each piece of pork.

note You can, of course, use pork belly from any breed of pig for this dish.

Lamb Marinated in Miso

Lamb is rarely used in Japanese cooking, but in this recipe the miso marinade transforms the lamb into something very different and truly delicious.

sea salt and freshly ground black pepper
handful of dried gourd shavings (kanpyo, see page 251)
1 whole rack of lamb, French trimmed (6 chops, see left)
Spicy Miso (page 245)
a little olive oil
3 white asparagus spears
3 heads of baby bok choy
3 garlic shoots (see page 250)
3 tablespoons Spicy Lemon Dressing (page 242)

1   At least 6 hours ahead, bring a pan of water to a boil. Rub salt into the gourd shavings, rinse with cold water, and plunge into the boiling water for 2 minutes; drain well.

2   Trim off any excess fat from the lamb and wrap the exposed bones with the dried gourd. Place the rack meat in the miso, making sure the wrapped bones stick out clear of the liquid. Allow to marinate for 6 hours.

3   Heat the oven to 400°F and heat a broiler or barbecue. Heat an ovenproof skillet with some olive oil in it. Remove the lamb from the marinade and quickly brown it all over in the oil over high heat for 2 minutes, then transfer to the oven for 12 minutes to finish cooking, or 2 to 3 minutes longer, if you prefer it medium to well done.

4   Meanwhile, bring another pan of water to a boil. Brush the asparagus stalks with olive oil and season with salt and pepper. Cook under the broiler or on the barbecue until just tender. Blanch the bok choy quickly in the boiling salted water for 1 minute and the garlic shoots for 30 seconds, then drain.

5   Remove the lamb from the oven and transfer to a warm plate to rest for 2 minutes. Then cut into 6 chops and arrange on a serving dish. Place the broiled asparagus, bok choy, and garlic shoots neatly around the lamb and dress with the lemon dressing. Wrapping the bones with the dried gourd, as well as giving a Japanese look, allows your guests to pick up the chops with their fingers.

Roast Duck Breast with Orange Miso

Orange miso is the perfect accompaniment to this quick and simple duck dish.

serves 2

5 tablespoons Den Miso (page 244)

5 tablespoons fresh orange juice

grated zest from 2 oranges

5 to 7 ounces duck breast

olive oil

1³/4 ounces sugar snap peas

1³/4 ounces chanterelle mushrooms

sea salt and freshly ground black pepper

2 bamboo or banana leaves

1 whole orange, cut in half and the flesh scooped out

1   About 2 hours ahead, mix the miso, orange juice, and orange zest together in a nonreactive bowl and set 2 tablespoons aside. Trim any excess fat from the duck breast and score the remaining fat with a sharp knife, then cut it into 2 even-size pieces. Put the duck breast into the bowl of orange miso and let it marinate for 2 hours.

2   Toward the end of that time, heat the oven to 400°F. Heat some olive oil in an ovenproof skillet over high heat. Drain any excess miso from the duck breast halves and place them, skin side down, in the skillet. Cook for 2 minutes, then turn over and place in the oven for 8 minutes longer to finish cooking.

3   Season the sugar-snap peas and mushrooms with sea salt and pepper. Place a skillet over medium heat and quickly sauté in olive oil for 2 minutes, then drain.

4   Toast the bamboo or banana leaves over an open flame and place in the empty orange shells. Place the duck breast halves inside the leaf-lined orange and drizzle the reserved orange miso over. Decorate with the mushrooms and peas, and place on a suitable serving dish.

note   Cooking the duck breast fat side down helps to release excess fat from the skin and make it crisp.

Shabu Shabu with Iberian Pork

Shabu shabu means "swish, swish," the sound created by the thinly sliced meat being moved from side to side in the pot. It is said that this dish originated around the thirteenth century, as a way for Genghis Khan to feed his Mongolian army. The idea was that they would all gather around a boiling pot and dip thinly sliced meat in it, hence the quick cooking time to save precious fuel. The dish arrived in Japan in the twentieth century and is a national favorite. Now popular all over Asia, this is fast becoming popular in the West. Although this is an unusual technique and obviously not really sautéing, we've decided it fits best here in this chapter.

serves 4

7 ounces pork loin, preferably from Iberian black pigs
2 bunches of watercress
2 bunches of enoki mushrooms, trimmed
8 Chinese cabbage or Napa cabbage leaves
8 shiitake mushrooms, stems removed
3 1/2 ounces inaniwa noodles or tagliatelle
salt
3/4 cup Jalapeño Ponzu (page 245)
5 1/4-inch square piece of konbu (see page 251)

1 Trim off the outside fat and any sinew from the pork loin and place it in the freezer for 20 minutes. (This gets it really cold and firm, so it can be sliced more easily.)

2 On a large serving platter, arrange the watercress, enoki mushrooms, cabbage leaves, and shiitake mushrooms neatly in the middle of the dish.

3 Cut the pork loin into as near wafer-thin slices as possible and fold each slice in half. Arrange these overlapping around the edge of the serving platter, then cover and refrigerate until ready to serve.

4 Cook the noodles in boiling, salted water, then refresh with cold water and drain. Place on a separate serving dish in 4 separate neat piles. Put the ponzu in 4 separate dipping bowls.

5 When ready to cook, place a portable gas stove on a table and put a shabu shabu pot, a heatproof ceramic dish, or a shallow saucepan half-filled with water on top. Place the konbu in the water and bring to a boil. Once it is boiling, turn the heat down to a slow simmer and remove the konbu.

6 Place the platter of pork and vegetables on the table, together with the noodles and the 4 dipping bowls of ponzu.

7 To eat, pick up a piece of pork with your chopsticks, dip it into the boiling stock, and swish from side to side for 10 seconds; then dip it in the jalapeño-flavored ponzu and eat. Continue in this way, also cooking the mushrooms and vegetables of your choice (the vegetables will need to be left in the stock a little longer to cook) until the whole platter has been consumed.

8 Finally, place the noodles in the hot stock and eat these last.

note You can use any pork or beef for this dish, as well as scallops, shrimp, and fish, just as long as the pieces are small enough to cook quickly in the stock.

Sukiyaki, Nobu-Style

Sukiyaki is very popular in Japan and normally eaten in the winter months. It is a great meal to share family-style, where everybody sits around the table watching it cook. In Japan, the poached eggs are served raw in dipping cups and the beef is dipped into the raw egg before eating. Don't overboil the sauce, as it will be too strong; have a little hot water on hand, in case this happens.

serves 4

7 ounces kobe or wagyu beef or well-marbled rib or sirloin of beef

2/3 cup sliced onions

1 bunch of watercress

1 bunch of enoki mushrooms

3 1/2 ounces inaniwa noodles or tagliatelle

4 soft-poached eggs

sauce

3 tablespoons soy sauce

3 tablespoons mirin (Japanese rice wine, see page 252)

3 tablespoons sake

1 cup Dashi (page 17) or beef stock

3 tablespoons sugar

1   About half an hour ahead, make the sauce by mixing all the ingredients in a saucepan and warming slowly until all the sugar dissolves.

2   Trim off the outside fat and any sinew from the beef and place it in the freezer for 20 minutes. (This gets it really cold and firm, so it can be sliced easily.) Slice the beef as near to wafer-thin as possible, and fold each slice in half.

3   Place the onions in the bottom of a sukiyaki pan or similar shallow saucepan. Arrange the beef slices on the top of those, with the watercress and enoki mushrooms in the middle.

4   Cook the noodles in boiling, salted water, refresh with cold water, and drain. Place on a separate serving dish in 4 separate neat piles. Place each of the 4 poached eggs in each of 4 separate dipping bowls.

5   When ready to cook, place a portable gas stove on a table and put the sukiyaki pan, heatproof ceramic dish, or shallow saucepan on top. Turn on the gas and pour enough of the sauce to come up to the underside of the beef. Bring to a boil and then turn down to a simmer, stirring occasionally and adding more sauce if needed. When the beef is just cooked, turn off the gas and eat by dipping the beef and the vegetables into the soft poached egg in the dipping cup.

6   When all the meat has been eaten, turn on the gas again and place the noodles into the hot sauce (add more sauce if needed), and heat through and eat these last.

grill

Atlantic Cod, Halibut, and Salmon with Saikyo Miso

The Pacific black cod, or sablefish, with miso has become perhaps one of the most famous dishes at all of the Nobu restaurants. Here we use the same technique and cooking method with Atlantic cod, halibut, and salmon. Some of our customers like to squeeze fresh lemon juice over the top to balance out the sweetness of the saikyo miso, but this is a matter of personal taste.

serves 2

Saikyo Miso
6^1/$_2$ tablespoons sake
6^1/$_2$ tablespoons mirin (Japanese rice wine, see page 252)
^{3}/$_4$ cup sugar
10 ounces white miso paste (see page 253)

2 fresh cod, halibut, or salmon fillets, each about 4 ounces, still
   with the skin but any pinbones removed

garnish
cherry plum tomatoes on the vine (optional)
small, slender zucchini, ideally with their flowers attached,
   briefly blanched and refreshed (optional)

1 About 2 days ahead, make the miso. In a heavy-
bottomed nonreactive saucepan, bring the sake and mirin
to a boil, and continue to boil for 2 to 3 minutes to let the
alcohol evaporate.

2 Using a wooden spoon, stir in the sugar until it
dissolves, then slowly mix in the miso paste, a little at a
time. Cook over medium heat, stirring constantly so as
not to let the mixture burn, for 10 to 15 minutes.

3 Strain the mixture through a strainer to remove any
lumps, then let cool and chill until very cold.

4 Place the fish in a nonreactive container, pour a good
splash of the miso over each fillet, and let marinate for
1 to 2 days in the refrigerator.

5 When you want to cook the fish, heat a broiler or the
oven to 400°F. Place the fillets in the broiler pan or on a
nonstick baking sheet and cook under the broiler or in the
heated oven for 10 to 12 minutes, turning once if broiling,
until cooked through and golden on the outside.

6 Place on a serving dish and dress the plate with a
little extra saikyo miso and some cherry plum tomatoes
on the vine or small, slender zucchini.

Grilled Sea Trout with Fried Spinach

Crunchy spinach tempura makes a perfect foil for grilled sea trout enhanced with a spicy vinegar-based sauce.

serves 4

vegetable oil, for deep-frying
4 fresh sea trout fillets, each about 5 ounces
sea salt and freshly ground black pepper
32 baby spinach leaves, rinsed and well dried
flour, for dusting
1 recipe quantity of Tempura Batter (page 99)

Spicy-Sour Sauce
1 tablespoon clarified butter (see page 126)
$1/2$ teaspoon chili-garlic sauce (see page 250)
$2/3$ cup Dashi (page 17)
2 tablespoons light soy sauce
2 tablespoons sake
$1/2$ teaspoon freshly ground black pepper
2 tablespoons rice vinegar
a little kuzu (see page 251) or cornstarch mixed with water

1   Heat a barbecue, or broiler, and heat half a small panful of oil for deep-frying to 350°F.

2   Lightly rub the trout fillets with a seasoning of salt and pepper, then cook on the barbecue grill, or under the broiler for 5 to 6 minutes, until just cooked through.

3   While the trout is cooking, dust the spinach leaves in flour and carefully dip one side only of each leaf in the tempura batter. Cook in small batches in the oil, draining them on paper towels.

4   Make the sauce by slowly melting the butter, if necessary, then add the chili-garlic sauce and cook for a few seconds. Add the Dashi and bring to a boil. Add the soy sauce, sake, and pepper, then finish with the rice vinegar and bring back just to a boil. Thicken slightly with the kuzu or cornstarch mixture and remove from the heat.

5   To serve, divide the spinach leaves among 4 plates, arranging them like the petals of a flower. Put a trout fillet next to them and spoon a little of the sauce around the fish.

note   As there is more than one cooking process involved in this dish and the timing is crucial to keep the spinach tempura crisp, it might be easier for two people to help in its preparation.

Mackerel Shio-Yaki and Vegetable Salad

This is a very simple way with mackerel—the succulent flesh is enhanced by the crunchiness of the vegetables and the sherry vinegar dressing. *Shio-yaki* is a traditional Japanese method of cooking fish, poultry, or meat that involves salting and grilling.

serves 2

1 red bell pepper
1/4 cucumber
1 yellow zucchini
3 large Chinese cabbage leaves
2 boneless, skin-on fresh mackerel fillets
sea salt and freshly ground black pepper
1/4 cup olive oil
2 tablespoons sherry vinegar

1   Cut the pepper in half and remove the stalk and the seeds, then cut the flesh into 1/4-inch dice and place in a mixing bowl. Cut the cucumber in half and remove the seeds with a spoon, then cut into 1/4-inch dice and add to the mixing bowl. Top and tail the yellow zucchini and cut lengthwise into 1/4-inch-thick strips, then into 1/4-inch dice; add to the bowl. Lay the cabbage leaves flat on top of one another and cut into 1/4-inch strips, then into 1/4-inch dice; add to the bowl.

2   Heat a barbecue grill or broiler and the oven to 350°F. Season the mackerel fillets with salt and pepper, and brush with a little of the olive oil. Place the fillets, skin side to the heat, on the barbecue or broiler pan, and cook for 1 minute on each side. Transfer to a baking dish and cook in the oven for 6 minutes longer.

3   Add the sherry vinegar and remaining olive oil to the diced vegetables and toss together. Season with salt and pepper to taste, then put on a serving dish and top with the cooked mackerel fillets.

 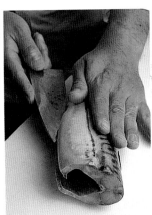  

Toro Steak with Balsamic Teriyaki Sauce

You will probably be amazed at just how sweet and subtly flavored roasted garlic can be, and here it makes the perfect accompaniment to lightly seared toro (tuna belly) steak.

serves 2

1 whole head of garlic
2 fresh toro (tuna belly) fillets, each about 3^1/$_2$ ounces
sea salt and freshly ground black pepper
Balsamic Teriyaki Sauce (page 247), warmed through
handful of fresh baby shiso leaves (see page 253)
handful of daikon cress (kaiware, see page 251)

1   Heat the oven to 350°F. Trim the root and the head of the garlic and remove any loose outside skin but keep the head intact. Wrap in foil, place in a baking dish, and roast for 20 minutes.

2   While the garlic is roasting, heat a barbecue grill or broiler. Season the tuna fillets with salt and pepper and briefly sear each of them on all the sides for 2 to 3 minutes, keeping the middle rare.

3   To serve, spoon a little of the hot sauce on each of 2 plates, then cut each tuna steak and the roasted garlic in half. Place the tuna steak halves in the middle of each plate and garnish with the shiso leaves and daikon cress, and a roasted garlic half.

Grilled Venison with Salted Plums and Wasabi

Here, fiery wasabi and salted plums are brought together to marry with grilled venison. In Japan, wasabi and salted plum is a favorite combination and it makes a perfect accompaniment for this dish.

serves 2

4 baby beets, trimmed
4 venison loin steaks, each about 3 ounces
sea salt and freshly ground black pepper
olive oil, for brushing
4 cep (porcini) mushrooms, halved
1 bunch of watercress, stems removed

Wasabi Pepper Sauce
1¹/2 teaspoons wasabi powder (see page 253)
1 tablespoon water
2¹/2 teaspoons soy sauce
2¹/2 teaspoons light soy sauce
3 tablespoons plus 1 teaspoon Dashi (page 17)
1 teaspoon freshly ground black pepper

Wasabi Plum Sauce
8 whole umeboshi (Japanese salted plums, see page 253)
1 tablespoon clarified butter (see page 126)
¹/2 clove garlic, thinly sliced
2 tablespoons sake
6¹/2 tablespoons Wasabi Pepper Sauce (above)

1   Heat a barbecue grill or broiler. Blanch the baby beets in boiling, salted water; they should still be al dente. Using paper towels, wipe the outside skin off the beets, then cut them into halves or quarters, depending on their size. (You will need to wear rubber gloves to prevent staining to your hands.)

2   Season the venison steaks with salt and pepper, and brush with a little olive oil.

3   To make the wasabi pepper sauce, put the wasabi powder in a bowl and mix with the water. Cover with plastic wrap and let stand for 10 minutes to allow the flavor to develop. Add the other ingredients and mix well.

4   To make the wasabi plum sauce, keeping 2 of the umeboshi separate for garnish, remove the pits from the other 6 and roughly chop the flesh. Place a skillet over medium heat, then add the butter and garlic. When the aroma of the garlic is released, add the chopped umeboshi and cook for a minute longer, keeping the temperature low so the garlic doesn't brown. Add the sake and bring to a boil, then add the pepper sauce and bring back to a boil. Remove from the heat immediately (or the wasabi will lose its pungency), season with salt and pepper, and keep warm.

5   Place the venison steaks on the barbecue or under the broiler and cook for 2 to 3 minutes on each side, depending on their thickness (they need to be still pink in the middle).

6   At the same time, season the mushroom halves and the blanched baby beets with salt and pepper, then barbecue or broil for 2 to 3 minutes until cooked.

7   Arrange the venison, ceps, and beets on 2 plates, spoon a little of the wasabi plum sauce around, and garnish with watercress and the whole umeboshi.

note   Although everybody seems to refer to umeboshi as a Japanese salted plum, it is, in fact, a salted apricot.

rice, sushi, and noodles

Nobu-Style Paella

In this recipe you can use any selection of your favorite fish or shellfish. We sometimes make this dish for the staff when we have an assortment of fish trimmings at the end of the day.

serves 4 to 6

large pinch of saffron threads
heaped 3 cups Japanese rice
4 to 6 baby octopus
4 to 6 small squid
4 to 6 shelled scallops
4 to 6 Mediterranean shrimp in the shell
4 to 6 langoustines in the shell
4 to 6 clams in the shell
1 2/3 cups Dashi (page 17)
sea salt and freshly ground black pepper
8 to 12 morel mushrooms
4 to 6 cep (porcini) mushrooms
2/3 cup podded fresh green peas
2/3 cup podded and skinned fresh fava beans

1   Lightly toast the saffron threads under a broiler for a few seconds until they become slightly darker. (This enables them to impart more color and flavor to the rice.)

2   Rinse the rice and leave it in cold water to soak for a while, then drain.

3   Prepare the seafood, scrubbing shells, removing beards, etc., and discard any shellfish that stays open when tapped.

4   Place the rice, saffron, Dashi, salt, and pepper in a flameproof, heavy earthenware pot that has a tight-fitting lid. Add the rest of the ingredients, then place the lid on top and set over high heat. Turn the heat down to medium just before it boils and cook for 10 minutes, then turn down the temperature to very low and cook for 10 minutes longer.

5   Finally, turn up the heat to high for 30 seconds, then remove from the heat and let the paella rest for 10 minutes before serving.

note   A wonderful addition to this dish is a little sprinkling of bonito flakes (see page 250) on the top when serving, as this gives it a slightly smoky flavor.

Parmesan Rice

This dish is very simple to make, but very rewarding, as it has the wonderful heady aroma of white truffle and is full of umami flavor.

serves 4

heaped 3 cups Japanese rice
1²/₃ cups Dashi (page 17)
1 cup freshly grated Parmesan cheese
white truffle, to serve

1   Rinse the rice well in cold water and leave to soak in fresh cold water for 20 minutes, then drain.

2   Put the rice, Dashi, and Parmesan into a flameproof earthenware dish with a tight-fitting lid, mix them together well, and place the lid on top. Set the dish over high heat, turn the heat down to medium just as it comes to a boil, and cook for 15 minutes. Turn the heat down to low and cook for 10 minutes longer, making sure the lid is not removed during the cooking process.

3   Remove from the heat and allow to stand for 5 minutes with the lid still on.

4   Just before serving, remove the lid from the dish and slice the white truffle thinly over the top of the rice. Scoop the rice into bowls at the table.

note   For the best results, make sure that you use good-quality Parmesan and that you grate it just before you mix it into the rice.

Rice Pizza

This Nobu version of pizza makes ideal finger food or can even be served as a light lunch. The amounts given here make three pizza crusts, but you can store/freeze the other two crusts for another day. With this dish there are countless combinations for the toppings or you can just stick to one type.

The dough for the crust is very elastic and must be well rested, or it will shrink during cooking.

Be sure to serve the pizza fairly quickly after making it, so the crust does not get the chance to become too soggy from the liquid in the toppings.

Mochi flour is milled from mochi rice, a short-grained, glutinous rice. It is used to thicken sauces, as well as for breading foods for frying and for making traditional desserts and cakes, or rice dumplings known as Japanese *mochi*.

makes 3 small pizza crusts and toppings for 1

crusts

1 1/2 cups mochi flour (Japanese rice flour, see page 252), plus more for dusting

pinch of salt

1 tablespoon olive oil, plus more for cooking

1 1/4 cups plus 4 teaspoons boiling water

toppings

2 teaspoons salmon eggs

2 teaspoons caviar

1 slice (1/3 ounce) of smoked salmon

1 slice (1/3 ounce) of cooked lobster

1 slice (1/3 ounce) of pickled herring

1 slice (1/3 ounce) of cooked crab claw meat

garnish

finely shredded daikon

shiso leaves (see page 253)

cilantro leaves

chervil leaves

bonito flakes (see page 250)

1   Put the mochi flour, salt, and olive oil into the bowl of a food processor. Turn it on, pour in the boiling water, and mix to a smooth dough. Turn out onto a floured board and let rest for 1 hour.

2   Divide the dough into 3 pieces (there is enough to make 3 crusts) and roll one piece out as thinly as possible into a circle. Let it rest in the refrigerator for 20 minutes. Store or freeze the remaining crusts for another time.

3   Heat a nonstick skillet over medium heat. Add 1 1/2 teaspoons of olive oil and fry the crust in the pan, turning it frequently and adjusting the temperature to prevent burning, for 2 to 3 minutes until light and golden. When cooked, turn out onto a clean chopping board and let cool, then cut into 6 equal wedges.

4   Place each of the 6 different toppings onto one of each of the 6 wedges and place the shredded daikon in the middle. Decorate each slice with the garnish of your choice and serve.

Sushi Rice (Shari)

Getting your sushi rice right is a crucial element in successful sushi-making. The preparation of the rice is so important that most sushi establishments in Japan have chefs whose sole responsibility is to cook the rice. One secret is always to measure your ingredients very carefully.

makes 5 cups

Sushi Vinegar (Shari Zu)
1 cup red Japanese vinegar (regular Japanese rice vinegar will do)
2 tablespoons plus 2 teaspoons sea salt
1 tablespoon mirin (Japanese rice wine, see page 252)
3/4 cup superfine sugar
about 1 1/2-inch square piece of konbu (see page 251)

3 2/3 cups Japanese short-grain rice
1 quart cold water

1   First, make the vinegar, which can be made well in advance and will keep in the refrigerator for up to a month. In a nonreactive saucepan, gently heat 2/3 cup of the vinegar with the salt, mirin, and sugar until the sugar completely dissolves—but do not let the liquid boil! Wipe the konbu with a clean, damp cloth to remove any residue and add to the liquid. Remove from the heat and let cool completely. When cold, add the remaining 1/3 cup vinegar. This quantity will be enough to make 2 batches of sushi rice.

2   In a large bowl of cold water, wash the rice, rubbing it and rinsing it frequently with fresh water until all the excess starch has gone and the water stops being cloudy and is clear. Soak in fresh cold water for about 30 minutes, then drain in a strainer.

3   To a heavy-bottomed saucepan, add the rice and the quart of water. Bring to a boil over high heat for 1 minute, then reduce the heat to low and continue cooking for 5 minutes longer. Lastly, return the heat to high for 10 seconds, then remove the pan from the heat. Let it sit for 15 minutes, then drain off any excess water.

4   Transfer the hot rice to a wooden Japanese rice tub or wide, shallow container and spread out thinly with a rice paddle or wide wooden spoon. Sprinkle half the sushi vinegar (about 2/3 cup) over the rice and, working quickly with the rice paddle in a slicing motion across the rice, cut through the rice from the bottom of the tub so it gets turned over and blends in the vinegar. Be careful not to squash or overstir the rice, or it will become too sticky. Cover with a clean, wet cloth and use while at room temperature within 1 hour. Do not let it become too cold or hard.

note   During the summer the rice will need less soaking, about 15 minutes.

Nigiri Sushi, European-Style

Professional sushi chefs train for years to perfect their technique, and although sushi made at home will never be on a par with that of a professional sushi chef, this is no reason not to try making it. The act of making it yourself will give you a great sense of accomplishment and is very rewarding—and lots of fun in the process. The more you practice, the better your understanding will be.

The easiest way to start is to stick to one type of fish until you get the hang of it and then progress to different types of fish. The two most important things to remember when making sushi are, first, that you buy only the freshest of fish (it should be no more than a day old) and, second, it should be eaten straightaway, as soon as it's made; never put it in the refrigerator for later. You should, of course, ensure that your hands, chopping board, and utensils are scrupulously clean.

When eating sushi, you should have the barest minimum of soy sauce in your dipping bowl so as not to swamp the sushi in it, and the fish side should be dipped into the soy sauce, not the rice, otherwise the rice will disintegrate and end up in the dipping bowl. There is no need to mix wasabi into the soy sauce, as it has already been added when the sushi was being made.

There are numerous combinations of sushi ingredients, from raw and cooked fish and shellfish to meat and vegetables. The following list is by no means exhaustive, but is here as a basic guide:

tuna; sea bass; turbot; snapper; sea bream; flounder; shelled cooked shrimp; salmon; salmon eggs; caviar; smoked fish, such as salmon, eel, or mackerel; cured fish, such as gravlax or pickled herring; squid; scallops; cooked lobster; cooked crab; sea urchin; seared foie gras; seared wagyu beef; broiled mushrooms.

serves 4 (about 24 nigiri sushi pieces)

hand vinegar (Tezu)
3 tablespoons water
1 tablespoon rice vinegar

about 14 ounces skinned fresh fish fillet or other topping
2 cups of Sushi Rice (page 194)
1 tablespoon wasabi
pickled ginger (gari, see page 250), to serve
soy sauce, for dipping

1 On a clean cutting board, place the fish fillet horizontally with the skin side up and the tail on the side of the preferred hand. Hold the knife in your preferred hand so the top is inclined away from the fish, and from the other side of the fillet start cutting thin slices (about 1/4 inch thick), keeping the blade at an acute angle to achieve a clean cut across the grain. You can apply pressure with your nonpreferred hand to the outside of the fish to keep it firm, but care must be taken that you do not cut yourself. The fish is sliced in one drawing stroke, letting the weight of the knife do the work as you draw back the blade. Once all the fish has been sliced, cover with a clean, damp cloth.

2 Mix the ingredients for the hand vinegar together and place in a small bowl.

3 To make the nigiri sushi, dip your fingers into the hand vinegar and rub your palms together. This helps stop the rice from sticking to your hands. You should have a light covering of the hand vinegar—be careful, if you have too much, it will prevent the rice from sticking together.

4 Pick a little more than a tablespoon of rice with your preferred hand and shape it into a rectangle (about 1³/4 by ³/4 inches). Place the rice across the insides of the first joint of the fingers of your preferred hand and, with the index and middle fingers of your other hand, press the rice into a firmer rectangle shape (the pressure should be firm but gentle, so you don't mash the rice), then turn the rice over to apply equal pressure to the other side.

5 Pick up a slice of fish with the nonpreferred hand and place it across the first joints of the fingers in that hand, then smear a tiny amount of wasabi across the length of the slice, using the index finger of the preferred hand (while still holding the rice rectangle in the palm of that hand).

6 Place the rectangle of rice on top of the fish and press the rice and fish firmly together with the index and middle fingers of the preferred hand, then turn the sushi over to apply equal pressure to the other side.

7 Arrange the sushi on a serving dish and serve with pickled ginger and small dishes of soy sauce.

Bo Sushi with Herring

Bo sushi, also known as loaf or stick sushi, is an easier way to make sushi. The fish (or shellfish or vegetables) is placed on a sheet of konbu or nori seaweed and rolled around the rice. The finished rolls can be made a couple of hours in advance and then cut into pieces for eating.

serves 4

sea salt
4 fresh herrings, filleted
4 pieces of shiraita konbu (white konbu, see page 251)
16 caper berries
4 cups of Sushi Rice (page 194)
4 teaspoons toasted sesame seeds
bamboo or banana leaves, to serve
pickled ginger (gari, see page 250), for garnish
soy sauce, for dipping

marinade for the herring
2/3 cup rice vinegar
5 tablespoons water
1 tablespoon superfine sugar
1 tablespoon light soy sauce

marinade for the konbu
6 tablespoons water
6 tablespoons rice vinegar
1 tablespoon light soy sauce

1   Sprinkle a little sea salt on both sides of the herring fillets and let them stand for 30 minutes.

2   Wash off the salt and pat the fillets dry. Mix all the ingredients for the herring marinade together and immerse the fillets in the marinade. Let stand for 10 minutes, then drain and pat dry.

3   Place the konbu marinade ingredients in a flat, wide pan and add the sheets of konbu. Simmer very slowly over low heat for 20 minutes, or until they become soft and translucent. Let cool in the liquid, then trim each sheet to the same size as the herring fillets.

4   Remove the stems from 8 caper berries and roughly chop them, then fold into the sushi rice, along with the sesame seeds.

5   To assemble, place a large sheet of plastic wrap on a chopping board and lay a sheet of konbu horizontally in the middle. Place a herring fillet on top of the konbu, skin side down, and then arrange 1 cup of sushi rice along the length of the fillet. Wrap the end of the plastic wrap nearest you over the top of the rice and roll the loaf up. Grabbing the ends of the plastic wrap, keep rolling the loaf on the surface of the chopping board so the contents inside the plastic wrap become tight and firm, resembling a sausage shape. Repeat the whole process for the remaining konbu and herring fillets.

6   When ready to serve, remove the plastic wrap from the loaves and place them on a clean chopping board. With a sharp knife, cut each loaf across into slices about 3/4 inch thick and arrange on a suitable serving dish atop bamboo or banana leaves. Garnish with the remaining caper berries and pickled ginger, and serve soy sauce separately for dipping.

note   This dish can also be made using mackerel, but you need to salt the mackerel for 1 hour and peel off the skin after marinating.

Freshwater Eel and White Truffle Egg Roll

The sweetness of the eel and the delicacy of the sushi omelet, combined with white truffle, make this a very special dish. Unagi kabayaki, ready-grilled freshwater eel, is very popular in Japan and readily available at Japanese food stores. When opening the packs of eel, reserve the tasty juices, which we spoon onto the plate under the rolls.

serves 2

4 extra-large eggs
1/4 cup Dashi (page 17)
1 1/2 tablespoons sugar
1 teaspoon salt
1 teaspoon soy sauce
3 1/2 ounces grilled freshwater eel (unagi kabayaki, see above)
olive oil, for frying
a little sliced white truffle

1 In a nonreactive bowl, beat together the eggs, Dashi, sugar, salt, and soy sauce, then strain through a fine strainer.

2 Heat a broiler. Chop the eel into chunks and broil for 1 to 2 minutes to warm through.

3 Place a well-greased square Japanese omelet pan (*tamago*) over low heat and pour in about one-quarter of the egg, then spread it evenly by tilting, as if making a French crepe. As it bubbles and begins to cook and set, roll it up toward the back of the pan (away from you), then grease the pan again with paper towels dipped in olive oil.

4 Pour in another quarter of the egg, ensuring it goes underneath the first roll, and cook in the same way as the first. Roll the first omelet at the back of the pan over the top of the second toward the front of the pan and then push the whole roll to the back. Oil the pan again and repeat until all the egg has been used. When cooking the last omelet, add the eel and truffle to the back end and roll everything up again to the front of the pan.

5 Turn the roll out onto a bamboo sushi mat and roll up in the mat like a sushi roll, squeezing out any excess juices, then leave to cool.

6 When cool, slice the roll into rounds about 3/4 inch thick and serve on a suitable dish.

note The temperature of the pan is crucial to making this dish—the heat should be low enough so the egg cooks and sets very slowly. Try practicing a few times to get the feel of how hot the pan should be; intermittently removing the pan from the heat is a good way to slow the cooking process.

Chicken and Prawn Spicy Garlic Don

Don or *donburi* is a typical Japanese dish of rice, topped with various ingredients. In this version, chicken and prawns are given a fiery kick by the addition of chili and garlic.

serves 1

3 ounces boneless, skinless chicken breast, thinly sliced
cornstarch, for dusting
olive oil, for frying
3 ounces fresh shelled tiger prawns
4 small broccoli florets
4 oyster mushrooms
3 asparagus spears, cut into 1¼-inch pieces
½ teaspoon chili-garlic sauce (see page 250)
2 tablespoons sake
2 tablespoons Sake Soy (page 248)
a little kuzu (see page 251) or cornstarch mixed with water to thicken
freshly ground black pepper
1 teaspoon toasted sesame oil
cooked rice, to serve

1 Dust the chicken breast lightly with cornstarch and sauté quickly in a little olive oil over high heat in a nonstick skillet for 1 to 2 minutes, until cooked through; remove from the pan and keep warm.

2 Repeat the process for the prawns, broccoli, oyster mushrooms, and asparagus one at a time, using the same pan and adding to the chicken as they are cooked.

3 Again using the same pan, quickly sauté the chili-garlic sauce for a few seconds and then deglaze the pan with sake. Add the Sake Soy and, just as it comes to a boil, thicken with the kuzu mixture, then quickly toss the chicken and vegetables into the sauce. Season with the black pepper and add the sesame oil at the last minute.

4 Place the cooked rice in a bowl, spoon the mixture on top, and enjoy.

notes When making this dish, make sure you have all the ingredients ready at the start, as it is basically a stir-fry and needs to be cooked quickly over high heat.
Try different combinations of meat and fish, or just vegetables, as the sauce goes well with anything.

New-Man Pasta

Hot noodles in broth are always a favorite, but in this dish we have substituted Italian pasta for noodles to give it a Western twist.

serves 2

fish broth
2 cups Dashi (page 17) or clear fish stock
3 tablespoons light soy sauce
1/2 teaspoon salt
2 tablespoons sake

vegetable oil, for deep-frying
2 cloves garlic, thinly sliced
3 1/2 ounces tagliolini or other flat, long pasta noodles
2 boneless fresh red snapper fillets, each about 3 1/2 ounces
olive oil, for frying and for brushing the fillets
sea salt and freshly ground black pepper
1 1/2 cups mixed mushrooms, such as shiitake, oyster, cep (porcini), and/or chanterelle
8 green olives
snipped fresh chives, for garnish

1 Make the fish broth by mixing all the ingredients together in a pan and heat slowly—do not boil.

2 Bring about 3/4 inch of oil in a saucepan to a temperature of 300°F and slowly deep-fry the garlic slices until they turn a light golden brown; remove immediately and drain on paper towels.

3 Cook the pasta in salted, boiling water until just al dente and drain.

4 Heat a broiler. Brush the snapper fillets with olive oil and season with salt and pepper. Cook under the broiler for 4 to 5 minutes, until just cooked through.

5 At the same time, season the mushrooms with salt and pepper and sauté in olive oil in a skillet over medium heat.

6 To serve, quickly reheat the pasta in boiling water for a few seconds, then drain and divide between 2 large noodle bowls. Add the mushrooms and olives and place the snapper fillets on the top. Pour the hot fish broth over the top and sprinkle with chives and the fried garlic.

note Try to get all the ingredients ready at the same time; if not, broil the fish last, so it doesn't overcook.

Tuna with Angel Hair Pasta

Here raw tuna is cut into thin strips, seasoned with sesame, chili, and garlic, and mixed with cold cooked angel hair pasta to make a really interesting combination.

serves 4

3 ounces angel hair pasta (capelli d'angelo)
salt
5 ounces boneless, skinless fresh tuna
2 tablespoons toasted sesame oil
2 tablespoons olive oil
1 teaspoon chili-garlic sauce (see page 250)
2 tablespoons soy sauce
1/2 bunch of chives, finely snipped

1   Cook the angel hair pasta in plenty of salted, boiling water until just al dente. Drain and refresh in cold water, then drain well again.

2   Following the grain of the tuna, slice it into long strips as thin as you can manage ($1/16$ to $1/8$ inch).

3   Combine with the drained pasta in a mixing bowl. Add the sesame and olive oils and gently mix again. Add the chili-garlic sauce to the soy sauce and gently mix into the salad, taste, and add a little more salt if required.

4   Place on a serving dish and sprinkle with the chives.

desserts

Ice Cream Tempura

Hot and cold, and soft and crispy, these are the exciting textures and contrasts this dessert presents. The measurements for this are only a rough guide, as it is more of a technique.

serves 2

4 scoops of ice cream in any of your favorite flavors
2 tablespoons cake crumbs
clean, unused vegetable oil, for deep-frying
flour, for dusting
small quantity of Tempura Batter (page 99)
confectioners' sugar, for dusting
bamboo leaf, to serve (optional)

1 First, scoop the ice cream into balls and then roll these in the cake crumbs until the outside is completely coated. Place back in the freezer for 2 to 3 hours to harden completely.

2 Heat a medium-to-large pan of clean oil ($3^3/_4$ to 4 inches deep) to a temperature of 350°F. Remove the ice cream balls from the freezer and quickly roll in the flour and then dip in the tempura batter, making sure the ice cream is completely covered. Place the battered ice cream balls gently into the oil (only cook 2 or 3 at a time, so the oil remains hot) and cook for 1 minute per batch, just until the batter is light and crisp. Remove and drain on paper towels.

3 Quickly place on a suitable dish, dust with confectioners' sugar, and serve immediately, on a bamboo leaf if you like.

note The secret to this dish is to have everything on hand when you are about to fry the ice cream. Two people can make quicker work of the frying, as the ice cream melts quickly, so it needs to be served as soon as possible after cooking.

Mochi Ice Cream

The wonderful contrast in texture between the soft and chewy sweet mochi balls and their ice cream filling makes this dessert a very special experience. Unusually, in this recipe we measure the water by weight for precision.

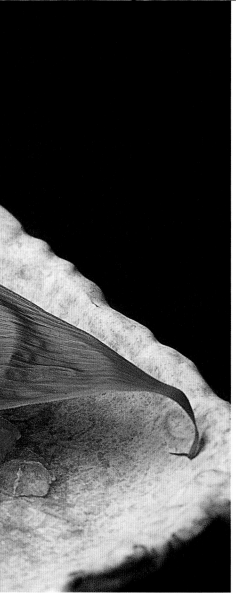

6 tablespoons plus 1 teaspoon superfine sugar
7 1/2 ounces water
1 cup less 1 tablespoon mochi flour (Japanese rice flour,
  see page 252)
cornstarch, for dusting
1 3/4 cups (14 ounces) good-quality ice cream, any flavor(s),
  softened in the refrigerator for 20 minutes

to serve
fresh bamboo leaves, crushed ice, and fresh seasonal berries

1   In a microwavable bowl, dissolve the sugar in the water
and mix in the mochi flour, ensuring there are not any
lumps. Cook in the microwave oven on medium heat for 30
seconds. Remove and beat vigorously with a wooden spoon
(the mix will become stiff and elastic). Place back in the
microwave oven and repeat the process 3 more times. Turn
out onto a board dusted with cornstarch and let cool.

2   Scoop the ice cream into small balls using a melon baller
(maximum diameter 3/4 inch) and place back in the freezer.

3   When the paste is cool, roll it out into a sheet about
1/8 inch thick, dusting it with cornstarch to prevent
sticking. Place on a tray and freeze for about 30 minutes
to harden.

4   Remove the mochi paste sheet from the freezer and,
using a 1 3/4- to 2-inch round cutter, cut out as many circles
as you can. Place an ice cream ball in the middle of each and
wrap it in the mochi paste, then place back in the freezer.

5   About 3 to 5 minutes before serving, remove the balls
from the freezer to allow the mochi to soften slightly.

6   Serve on bamboo leaves set on top of a plate of
crushed ice and decorate with fresh seasonal berries.

note   Make green tea- or chocolate-flavored mochi by
replacing 1 1/2 tablespoons of mochi flour with green tea
powder or unsweetened cocoa powder.

Chocolate Satandagi

This consists of a very light doughnut with a soft chocolate middle, served with almond ice cream. It might be an idea to warn your guests to be careful when eating the satandagi, as the chocolate inside the doughnut is very liquid.

serves 4 to 6

Almond Ice Cream
7 ounces heavy cream
7 ounces milk
5 egg yolks
5 tablespoons superfine sugar
1 2/3 cups finely ground blanched almonds

Chocolate Ganache
5 ounces semisweet chocolate (about 66% cocoa solids)
2/3 cup heavy cream

batter
2 egg yolks
1/4 cup superfine sugar
1/2 cup plus 1/2 to 1 tablespoon milk
1 cup flour
whites of 3 eggs

vegetable oil, for deep-frying
shelled pistachio nuts, to serve
raspberry puree, to decorate (optional)

1 To make the ice cream, heat the cream and milk to just below the boiling point. Whisk the egg yolks and sugar together in a large bowl. Pour the hot milk and cream mixture on the egg yolks and sugar, whisking continuously, then return to a clean saucepan. Cook over gentle heat, stirring continuously, until the mixture begins to thicken slightly: do not let it boil or the egg yolks will be scrambled in the custard. Remove from the heat, whisk in the ground almonds, and let cool completely. Strain the mixture into an ice-cream machine and freeze according to the manufacturer's directions.

2 To make the ganache, break the chocolate into small chunks and place in a heatproof bowl. Heat the cream in a saucepan to just below the boiling point and remove from the heat. Pour the cream on the chocolate and stir gently to mix in as the chocolate melts. Leave the ganache to cool, then refrigerate. When cold, scoop into tablespoon-size pieces and place in the freezer to freeze solid.

3 To make the batter, whisk 2 egg yolks with 1 1/3 tablespoons superfine sugar in a large bowl. Whisk in the milk, followed by the flour, a little at a time, making sure there are not any lumps. In another large bowl, whisk the egg whites and the remaining 2 tablespoons of sugar to form a meringue, then fold this lightly into the batter mixture.

4 Heat a medium-to-large pan of oil (3 3/4 to 4 inches) to a temperature of 325°F. Place a bamboo skewer into each of the frozen ganache scoops, then use the skewer to dip the ganache into the batter, making sure it is completely covered. Dip into the hot oil and cook for 2 minutes, then remove and drain on paper towels.

5 Transfer to a suitable serving dish and serve with the almond ice cream and sprinkled with pistachio nuts. If you like, you can give the plate a dash of color with a few splashes of raspberry puree.

note You can make the chocolate ganache well in advance and store in the freezer.

Chestnut Brûlée with Chocolate Sorbet and Tonka Bean Foam

Here a brûlée of chestnut-flavored cream is complemented by a rich, dark chocolate sorbet and finished with an aromatic tonka bean foam.

serves 6

Tonka Bean Foam
2 extra-large egg yolks
2 medium egg whites
1/4 cup sugar
1/2 cup milk
1/2 cup whipping cream
5 tonka beans (see page 253)
1 teaspoon nibbed cocoa
1/2 vanilla bean
1/2 leaf gelatin

Chocolate Sorbet
7 ounces semisweet chocolate (minimum 70% cocoa solids)
1 cup plus 2 tablespoons water
1/2 cup plus 2 tablespoons sugar
2 tablespoons plus 1 teaspoon liquid glucose

Chestnut Brûlée
2 medium egg yolks
2 tablespoons superfine sugar
6 1/2 tablespoons heavy cream
3/4 cup plus 2 tablespoons chestnut puree

to decorate
Dried Apple Slices (page 232)
marrons glacés

1   To make the foam, whisk the egg yolks, whites, and the sugar together in a bowl. Place the milk, cream, tonka beans, and cocoa nibs in a saucepan. Split the vanilla bean and scrape out the seeds, add these and the bean to the milk, and slowly heat until just boiling.

2   Pour the milk and cream mixture onto the egg and sugar, and whisk together. Return to the saucepan and cook over low heat until the mix thickens slightly, or reaches a maximum of 350°F, and remove from the heat.

3   Soak the gelatin in a little water, then add to the lukewarm mixture and leave to cool. When completely cold, whisk to a smooth liquid and place in a cream gun. Fill with gas according to the manufacturer's directions and refrigerate.

4   To make the sorbet, break the chocolate into small pieces and place in a large bowl. Warm the water, sugar, and glucose together in a saucepan until they dissolve and then heat to 350°F. Pour onto the chocolate and stir gently until the chocolate melts and is completely blended. Let the mixture cool, then churn in an ice-cream machine according to the manufacturer's directions; place in the freezer.

5   To make the brûlée, heat the oven to 375°F. Whisk together the egg yolks and sugar. Heat the cream in a saucepan to just below the boiling point and pour onto the eggs and sugar, whisking together. Blend the chestnut puree into the cream and egg mixture until completely smooth. Pour the mixture into suitable ovenproof serving dishes, place in a hot-water bath, and cook for 40 minutes. Remove and let cool, then refrigerate until ready to serve.

6   To serve, place a scoop of sorbet on the top of the brûlée, partly cover with the tonka bean foam, and garnish with some apple slices and marrons glacés.

note   If tonka beans are not available, replace them with vanilla and almond extracts, plus a pinch of cinnamon.

Apricot and Jasmine Soup with Peanut Crunch and Beer Ice Cream

This dessert has an unusual combination of a salted peanut crunch with an apricot sauce infused with jasmine. When eaten with the malty flavor of beer ice cream, it produces a wonderful range of flavor sensations.

serves 6 to 8

Apricot and Jasmine Soup
2 tablespoons sugar
2 tablespoons water
1 teaspoon jasmine tea
1 cup pureed peeled apricots

Beer Ice Cream
6¹/2 tablespoons heavy cream
2/3 cup milk
6 egg yolks
3/4 cup superfine sugar
1 cup beer (any malt or lager-type beer)

Peanut Crunch
6 tablespoons butter
2²/3 tablespoons superfine sugar
1/4 cup packed soft light brown sugar
5 tablespoons peanut butter
1/3 cup unsalted roasted peanuts
scant 1/2 cup unsalted roasted hazelnuts
1 teaspoon Maldon sea salt
1 teaspoon baking powder
1 cup bread flour

to decorate
Dried Apple Slices (page 232)
fresh shiso leaves (see page 253)

1 You need to make the soup a day in advance. Warm the sugar with the water until the sugar dissolves, then mix with the jasmine tea. Whisk the apricot puree into the tea mixture and leave to infuse overnight.

2 To make the ice cream, heat the cream and milk to just below the boiling point. Whisk the egg yolks and sugar together in a large bowl. Pour the hot milk and cream mixture onto the egg yolks and sugar, whisking continuously, then return to a clean saucepan. Cook over gentle heat, stirring continuously, until the mixture begins to thicken slightly: do not let it boil or the egg yolks will be scrambled in the custard. Remove from the heat and let cool.

3 Mix the beer into the mixture, place in an ice-cream machine, and freeze according to the manufacturer's directions.

4 To make the peanut crunch, soften the butter and cream together in a mixing bowl with the superfine sugar, brown sugar, and peanut butter. Gently mix in the rest of the ingredients, roll up the mix in plastic wrap, and chill until set.

5 Heat the oven to 350°F and cut the (now solid) peanut crunch dough into 1/2-inch-thick slices. Place on a nonstick baking sheet and bake for 8 to 12 minutes. Let cool, and break into rough chunks.

6 To serve, place a little of the peanut crunch in each serving bowl and top with a scoop of the ice cream. Strain a little of the soup into the bottom of the bowl and finish with a dried apple slice and a shiso leaf.

Nashi Pear Gyoza with Passion Fruit Sauce

These are essentially pot sticker dumplings with a sweet filling. In Japan, they are normally made with a savory filling, but they also make an excellent dessert. In this recipe, the filling is Asian pear combined with pecan nuts and fresh mint, and they are served with a passion fruit dipping sauce.

makes 16 to 20 (serves 3 to 4)

1/4 cup packed Demerara sugar

7 ounces Nashi Asian pears, peeled, cored, and diced

finely grated or pared zest of 2 lemons and juice of 1/2 lemon

1/4 cup shelled pecan nuts

10 fresh mint leaves

16 to 20 gyoza or wonton wrappers

1/2 cup passion fruit puree

olive oil, for cooking

2 to 4 drops of toasted sesame oil

1 Place the sugar, pears, and lemon zest and juice in a small bowl, cover with plastic wrap, and steam for 20 minutes. Remove the contents and strain off the liquid; let cool and keep aside.

2 Chop the pecan nuts and the mint, and stir these into the pear mix.

3 To make the gyoza, lay a gyoza or wonton wrapper in front of you, moisten the edge of the dough with a little water, put a spoonful of pear mix in the middle of each wrapper, and fold it over the top of the mix to make a semicircle. Seal the edge by making little folds and squeeze the ends together. Repeat the process until all the mix has been used.

4 Make the dipping sauce by mixing the juice left from the steaming of the pear with the passion fruit puree and a little water if too thick.

5 Place a small amount of olive oil in a nonstick saucepan over medium heat and cook the gyozas, flat end down, in the pan. When the bottom just begins to brown, add 3 tablespoons of water and 2 drops of sesame oil to the pan, turn the heat to high, and cover with a lid to let the gyoza steam for 2 to 3 minutes, until all the water evaporates. Repeat the process for any remaining gyoza.

6 Serve the gyoza on a suitable dish while still hot, with the brown side upright and a dipping bowl of the passion fruit puree.

note You can make different fillings for the dumplings using any hard fruits, such as pineapple, ordinary pear, or apple.

Summer Fruit Sake Gelatin Dessert

This dish is on the menus of our London restaurants when there is an abundance of berry fruit, and it makes a light and delightful end to a meal. It can be made with any of your favorite summer fruits—strawberries, wild strawberries, raspberries, black currants, red currants, or rowanberries.

makes 24 spoonful servings

3 1/2 ounces selection of summer berries
2 gelatin leaves
1/4 cup superfine sugar
6 1/2 tablespoons sake
fresh mint, for garnish

1   Wash the fruit gently, drain well, and place on paper towels to absorb the excess moisture.

2   Place the gelatin leaves in a nonreactive bowl and add 6 1/2 tablespoons water and the sugar. Warm the bowl gently, preferably over a saucepan of hot water, and stir slowly until all the sugar and gelatin dissolves; set aside to cool slightly.

3   When the mixture is tepid, stir in the sake and strain the mixture through a fine strainer to remove any remaining small lumps of gelatin.

4   Pour a little of the mixture into the base of the mold (see note opposite) or spoon to cover the bottom, and place in the freezer for a few minutes to set.

5   Remove the mold from the freezer, place the fruit on top of the set gelatin, and cover with the remaining gelatin mixture. Place in the refrigerator and allow to set for 3 to 4 hours.

6   When the gelatin is fully set, if using a mold, run a little warm water over the bottom of the mold and turn out onto your serving dish. Garnish with mint sprigs.

note   When we make these gelatins in the restaurant, we use a rubber mold designed for making mini chocolates (look for them in upscale cookwear stores and Internet sites). If you don't have access to something like this, you can use one big mold, as this makes it easier to turn out the gelatin. If you are using little molds, when unmolding, first place the desserts in the freezer to set a little harder, as this will help make them easier to turn out. Don't worry if they freeze, because after you have turned them out, the gelatin will become clear again as they defrost.

Plum Wine Tagliatelle

Japanese *Umeshu,* or plum wine, is made from a species of plum that actually has more resemblance to an apricot. It has a sweet, smooth flavor and in this recipe is set into a jelly almost like a cold sweet noodle.

serves 4

1 gelatin leaf
1 3/4 cups Japanese plum wine
4 teaspoons agar agar
fresh shiso sprigs (see page 253), to decorate

1   Soak the gelatin leaf in a little cold water for 2 minutes.

2   Mix the plum wine and agar agar in a small pan and bring just to a boil, then whisk in the gelatin leaf until it dissolves. Pour the mixture into a flat stainless-steel tray to a depth of about $1/8$ inch and put in the refrigerator to set for 3 to 4 hours. (Make sure the tray is level so the liquid sets to an even thickness.)

3   When ready to serve, remove the tray from the refrigerator and make cuts lengthwise with a pizza wheel or knife to produce strips of jelly that resemble tagliatelle. Wipe the underside of the tray with a cloth dipped in hot water to help loosen the tagliatelle and place in suitable bowls. Garnish with shiso sprigs.

notes   In summer, serve these as quickly as possible, as the noodles will melt.

You can sprinkle a little fruit juice or more plum wine on the tagliatelle when serving, if you like.

Agar agar, or *kanten* in Japan, is produced from seaweed and has a neutral smell and taste. It can be bought in powder form.

Whiskey Cappuccino

This dessert is layered with a wonderful array of textures and flavors, from an intense coffee brûlée and a cocoa crunch through to iced milk and cream, and then the luxurious topping of whiskey foam.

makes 8 cups

Iced Milk and Cream
1/4 cup sugar
1 tablespoon milk powder
3 tablespoons plus 1 1/2 teaspoons heavy cream
3/4 cup milk

Cocoa Crunch
1/4 cup sugar
3 tablespoons plus 1 teaspoon butter
1/2 cup ground almonds
1 teaspoon unsweetened cocoa powder
1/3 cup flour
2 teaspoons crushed coffee beans

Whiskey Foam
2/3 cup milk
2 tablespoons heavy cream
1 tablespoon plus 1 teaspoon sugar
2/3 gelatin leaf
3 tablespoons whiskey

Coffee Brûlée
9 medium egg yolks
1/4 cup sugar
3 tablespoons plus 3 teaspoons milk
3/4 ounce coffee paste, or 1 1/3 tablespoons plus 1 teaspoon triple-strength espresso coffee
7 ounces whipping cream

1   First make the iced milk and cream by mixing together the sugar, milk powder, cream, and milk in a saucepan. Bring to a boil over medium heat, then leave to cool slightly and liquidize for a few seconds; strain and refrigerate. When cold, churn in an ice-cream machine according to the manufacturer's directions.

2   For the cocoa crunch, beat together the sugar and butter until light and creamy. Fold in the almonds, followed by the rest of the ingredients, until completely incorporated. Then place the mixture in the freezer for 15 minutes, or until solid.

3   Heat the oven to 350°F. Grate the frozen cocoa crunch mixture onto a nonstick baking sheet no more than 1/8 inch in height and cook in the oven for 7 to 10 minutes; leave to cool, then break into rough chunks.

4   For the whiskey foam topping, bring the milk quickly to a boil with the cream and sugar, then remove from the heat. Soak the gelatin in a little cold water, then whisk it into the milk and cream mixture along with the whiskey, while it is still lukewarm; let set. When completely cold, whisk it into a smooth liquid and place in a cream gun. Fill with gas according to the manufacturer's directions.

5   For the brûlée, preheat the oven to 225°F, then whisk together the egg yolks and sugar in an ovenproof bowl. In a saucepan, bring the milk, coffee paste, and whipping cream just to a boil and then whisk into the egg yolks and sugar. Strain the mixture into 8 cappuccino cups, filling them only one-third of the way up, and place in a baking tray filled with hot water. Place in the oven for 25 minutes. When set, let cool, then refrigerate.

6   To serve, place a little of the cocoa crunch in each of the cups on top of the brûlée, followed by a scoop of the iced milk and cream. Top with the whiskey foam to resemble a cappuccino. Eat with teaspoons.

cocktails

Lychee Martini

This cocktail is best when it is served with a fresh lychee in it, and even better if served with the Thai Dragon lychee, when it is in season. If you can't find fresh lychees, any canned type can be substituted.

serves 1

1 ounce lychee liqueur
1 ounce vanilla vodka
1 ounce mandarin vodka
1/2 ounce passion fruit juice
splash of fresh lime juice
ice cubes
fresh or canned lychee, for garnish (see above)

1   Pour the liquids into a cocktail shaker full of ice cubes and shake well for 20 seconds.

2   Pour into a chilled martini glass and garnish with a lychee and serve.

Pineapple Martini

This refreshing summer martini is full of tropical pineapple flavor and has proved incredibly popular, especially with the ladies.

serves 1

1 ounce pineapple vodka
1 ounce peach schnapps
3/4 ounce pineapple puree
dash of fresh lemon juice
dash of sirop de gomme (sugar syrup)
ice cubes

1   Pour the liquids into a cocktail shaker full of ice cubes and shake well for 20 seconds.

2   Pour into a chilled martini or other suitable glass.

Apple Martini

This very popular version of the martini has a slightly sour twist to it that brings out the apple flavors. The dried apple slices are an optional extra, but they are also great on fruit salads or with ice cream.

serves 1

Dried Apple Slices (optional)
1 Granny Smith apple, cored but unpeeled
squeeze of fresh lemon juice

1 1/2 ounces sour apple schnapps
1 1/3 ounces vodka
3/4 ounce apple juice
good splash of fresh lime juice
ice cubes

1   If using the dried apple slices, you need to make them well ahead. Slice the apple across very thinly on a mandoline grater (the slices should be no more than $1/32$ inch thick) and place the slices in a bowl of water with a squeeze of lemon juice. Remove from the water and pat dry, then place on a nonstick baking sheet. Place the baking sheet in a very cool oven (225°F) and leave for around 6 hours, checking and turning at hourly intervals to make sure the slices dry uniformly but do not color.

2   To make the martini, pour the liquids into a cocktail shaker full of ice cubes, shake well for 20 seconds, and pour into a chilled martini glass. Garnish with a dried apple slice, if you like, and serve immediately.

Watermelon Martini

This very refreshing version of the martini uses fresh watermelon juice. Shochu is a Japanese clear liquor rather like vodka.

serves 1

1 ounce vodka
1/3 ounce shochu (see above)
1 ounce melon schnapps
1 ounce fresh watermelon juice (see note)
dash of sirop de gomme (sugar syrup)
dash of fresh lime juice
ice cubes
wedge of watermelon, for garnish

1   Place all the ingredients, except the watermelon, in a cocktail shaker and shake for 20 seconds.

2   Strain into a martini glass and garnish with a slice of watermelon.

note   The best way to make the watermelon juice is to chop up some watermelon flesh and place it in a cocktail shaker and press it with the end of a rolling pin to squeeze out the juice.

Tokyo Peach Cocktail

This is a simple and refreshing take on the classic Bellini.

serves 1

1/3 ounce Crème de Peche
3/4 ounce Calpico (see note)
1/3 ounce peach puree
chilled champagne to top off
ice cubes

1   Place all the ingredients, except the champagne, in a cocktail shaker with some ice cubes and shake for 20 seconds.

2   Strain into a champagne glass and top off with champagne.

note   Calpico is a concentrated cultured milk drink with a slightly citrusy flavor that is very popular in Japan. Japanese food stores sell this in cans.

Midori Margarita

The addition of Midori, a Japanese melon liqueur, makes this margarita very special. It does not, however, suit the normal garnish of salt.

serves 1

ice cubes
1 ounce Triple Sec
1 ounce Midori
1 ounce tequila
dash of fresh lime juice
lime wedge, for garnish

1   Place some ice cubes and all the liquids in a cocktail shaker and shake for 20 seconds.

2   Strain into a glass filled with ice cubes and garnish with a lime wedge.

Japanese Mojito

Our twist on the classic Cuban mojito uses vodka instead of rum, and fresh shiso leaves along with mint, together with a hint of vanilla, which creates an interesting flavor combination.

serves 1

3/4 ounce sirop de gomme (sugar syrup)
1 drop of vanilla extract
6 fresh shiso leaves
8 fresh mint leaves, plus more for garnish
1/2 ounce fresh lime juice
crushed ice
2 ounces vodka

1   Place the syrup, vanilla, and 4 shiso leaves in a blender and blend together.

2   Crush and mix together the remaining shiso leaves, mint leaves, and lime juice in a tall glass and fill with crushed ice.

3   Pour in the syrup mixture and the vodka, and stir.

Sake Mule

This twist on the classic '40s cocktail, using sake instead of vodka, has a spicy kick to it.

serves 1

1 slice of ginger
1/2 lemongrass stalk, plus another crushed stalk for garnish
2 fresh shiso leaves
2 ounces sake
splash of kalamansi juice (see page 251) or lime juice
1/3 ounce sirop de gomme (sugar syrup)
1/3 ounce elderflower cordial
dash of runny honey
crushed ice
splash of ginger beer

1   In a cocktail shaker, crush the ginger, lemongrass, and shiso leaves.

2   Add the rest of the ingredients, apart from the ginger beer, and shake.

3   Strain into a glass filled with more crushed ice, top off with the ginger beer, and garnish with the crushed lemongrass stalk.

notes   The kalamansi, or sour lime, looks like a green tangerine but has a very sour taste.

   Ginger beer has a more pronounced flavor than ginger ale. Look for it in stores selling food from the Caribbean. Elderflower cordial, so popular in England, however, might be difficult to source. Look for it on Internet sites selling British food products.

Japanese Bloody Mary

Our version of the classic Bloody Mary is made using wasabi instead of horseradish, to give it a subtly different kick.

serves 1

2 ounces vodka
1/3 ounce yuzu (see page 253) or fresh lemon juice
dash of Japanese tonkatsu sauce (see page 253) or
  Worcestershire sauce
1/2 teaspoon wasabi paste
freshly ground black pepper
tomato juice, to top off
ice cubes
cucumber wedge, for garnish
shiso leaf, for garnish

1   Mix together the vodka, yuzu or lemon juice, tonkatsu or Worcestershire sauce, wasabi, and black pepper to taste, then top off with tomato juice to taste.

2   Pour over ice cubes in a cocktail glass and garnish with the cucumber wedge and shiso leaf.

Orange Ki

This cocktail is a perfectly matched combination of orange, apple, almond, cinnamon, and whiskey, shaken with ice.

serves 1

2 orange wedges
1/2 teaspoon ground cinnamon
1/3 ounce sirop de gomme (sugar syrup)
1 ounce Jack Daniel's
1 ounce Amaretto
1 ounce fresh apple juice
crushed ice
dash of Kahlúa
1 cinnamon stick, for garnish

1   In a cocktail shaker, crush and mix together the orange wedges, ground cinnamon, and syrup.

2   Pour in the Jack Daniel's, Amaretto, and apple juice, and shake with crushed ice.

3   Strain into a glass filled with more crushed ice, pour a little Kahlúa on the top, and garnish with a cinnamon stick.

sauces

dressings

Jalapeño Dressing

2 teaspoons chopped jalapeño chili
1 teaspoon sea salt
1 teaspoon chopped garlic
6¹/2 tablespoons rice vinegar
1/2 cup grapeseed oil

1   In a food processor, process the jalapeño, salt, garlic, and vinegar until well mixed and the chili is finely chopped.

2   Slowly add the grapeseed oil and process until well blended.

Spicy Lemon Dressing

6¹/2 tablespoons fresh lemon juice
3 tablespoons plus 1 teaspoon soy sauce
1 heaped teaspoon finely chopped garlic
1/2 teaspoon chili-garlic sauce (see page 250)
1 teaspoon sea salt
1/2 teaspoon freshly ground black pepper
scant 2/3 cup grapeseed oil

1   In a bowl, mix together all the ingredients, except the oil, mixing well to dissolve the salt.

2   Mix in the oil.

Matsuhisa Dressing

1 cup finely chopped onion
1/4 cup plus 2 teaspoons soy sauce
2 tablespoons plus 1 teaspoon rice vinegar
1 teaspoon sugar
1/2 teaspoon Japanese or English powdered mustard
sea salt and freshly ground black pepper
4 teaspoons water
2 tablespoons plus 1 teaspoon toasted sesame oil
2 tablespoons plus 1 teaspoon grapeseed oil

1   Rinse the onion in cold water to remove the sharpness, then drain well.

2   In a mixing bowl, mix together the drained onion, soy sauce, vinegar, sugar, mustard powder, salt, pepper, and water.

3   When the salt dissolves, mix in the sesame and grapeseed oils, a little at a time.

note   This dressing develops a better flavor when made a day ahead of using.

Spicy Lemon and Caper Dressing

2 tablespoons salt-packed capers
6¹/₂ tablespoons Spicy Lemon Dressing (opposite)

1 Rinse the capers well under cold running water to remove the salt, then drain.

2 Finely chop the capers.

3 Mix well with the Spicy Lemon Dressing.

Watercress Dressing

1 ounce fresh watercress leaves and stems
1 heaped teaspoon salt
¹/₂ teaspoon freshly ground black pepper
¹/₄ cup rice vinegar
2 tablespoons grapeseed oil

1 Coarsely chop the watercress.

2 Place this and all the other ingredients in a food processor and blend.

salsas

Ginger Salsa

²/₃ cup finely chopped red onion
2 tablespoons finely chopped ginger
6¹/₂ tablespoons Tosa-Zu Sauce (page 31)

Combine all the ingredients and mix well.

Jalapeño Salsa

2 teaspoons finely chopped jalapeño chili
²/₃ cup finely chopped white onion
1 tablespoon plus 1 teaspoon olive oil
¹/₄ cup fresh lemon juice
²/₃ teaspoon salt

Combine all the ingredients and mix well.

sauces

Dashi Ponzu

3 tablespoons plus 1 teaspoon Dashi (page 249)
3 tablespoons plus 1 teaspoon Ponzu (page 248)

Combine the liquids together and mix well.

Yuzu Ponzu Dressing

5 tablespoons Ponzu (page 248)
1 tablespoon yuzu juice (see page 253)

Combine the ingredients together in a bowl and mix well.

Den Miso

6¹/2 tablespoons sake
6¹/2 tablespoons mirin
10 ounces white miso paste (see page 253)
³/4 cup sugar

1   Put the sake and mirin in a nonreactive saucepan and bring to a boil for 2 to 3 minutes to evaporate off the alcohol.

2   Over medium heat, add the miso paste to the pan a little at a time, to blend it into a smooth sauce.

3   Turn up the heat and add the sugar in 2 or 3 batches and continue stirring so the mixture does not burn.

4   When the sugar completely dissolves, remove the pan from the heat and leave the mixture to cool to room temperature. This will keep in the refrigerator for up to 3 months.

Shiso Ponzu

1 tablespoon green Tabasco sauce
1 tablespoon soy sauce
1 tablespoon shiso vinegar or rice vinegar
1 tablespoon grapeseed oil
1 tablespoon fresh lime juice
2 teaspoons finely chopped red chili
1¹/2 tablespoons finely chopped white onion
1 tablespoon finely chopped fresh shiso (see page 253) or cilantro leaves

Combine all the ingredients together in a bowl and mix well.

note   Only add the chopped shiso or cilantro leaf at the last minute, otherwise they will turn brown if added more than 20 minutes ahead of use.

Spicy Miso

6¹/₂ tablespoons sake
6¹/₂ tablespoons mirin
5 ounces red miso paste (see page 252)
5 ounces white miso paste (see page 253)
³/₄ cup sugar
¹/₂ teaspoon shichimi togarashi (see page 252)
2 tablespoons chili oil
1 tablespoon toasted sesame oil
6¹/₂ tablespoons water

1   Put the sake and mirin in a nonreactive saucepan and bring to a boil to evaporate off the alcohol.

2   Lower the heat to medium and add the miso pastes, a little at a time, and blend to a smooth sauce.

3   Turn up the heat and add the sugar in 2 or 3 batches, continuing to stir so the mixture does not burn. When the sugar completely dissolves, remove the pan from the heat and let the mixture cool to room temperature.

4   When cool, whisk in the shichimi, chili oil, sesame oil, and water just before using. This will keep in the refrigerator for up to 3 months.

Jalapeño Ponzu

6¹/₂ tablespoons Jalapeño Dressing (page 242)
6¹/₂ tablespoons Ponzu (page 248)

Mix the two ingredients well together in a bowl.

New-Style Oil

3 tablespoons light olive oil
1 teaspoon toasted sesame oil

Combine the two ingredients together.

note   This can be made ahead of time and will keep for up to a week, but once it has been heated, it should be discarded, because heating burns the sesame oil.

Red Anticucho Sauce

1/2 teaspoon dried oregano
2 tablespoons plus 1 teaspoon aji panca (Peruvian red chili paste, see page 250)
3 tablespoons plus 1 teaspoon rice vinegar
1 teaspoon finely chopped garlic
1 teaspoon ground cumin
2 tablespoons sake
1 teaspoon sea salt
1 teaspoon freshly ground black pepper
2 tablespoons grapeseed oil

1   Crush the oregano using a mortar and pestle to release its aroma.

2   Combine this with all the other ingredients, except the oil, and mix well until the salt dissolves.

3   Mix in the oil.

Spicy Sour Sauce

6 1/2 tablespoons fresh lemon juice
1 tablespoon soy sauce
2 teaspoons mirin
1 teaspoon chili-garlic sauce (see page 250)

Combine all the ingredients and mix well together.

Creamy Spicy Sauce

1 fresh egg yolk
1 teaspoon sea salt
pinch of freshly ground white pepper
1 teaspoon rice vinegar
6 tablespoons grapeseed or vegetable oil
1 teaspoon chili-garlic sauce (see page 250)

1   Put the egg yolk in a small bowl. Add the salt, white pepper, and rice vinegar and mix together.

2   Add the oil gradually, drop by drop at first but faster as you proceed, and whisk constantly.

3   Add the chili-garlic sauce and mix well.

note   You can use store-bought mayonnaise instead of making your own and simply mix that with chili-garlic sauce; if using fresh egg, only make it when it is needed and use it immediately.

Spicy Black Bean Sauce

1 tablespoon black bean paste
5 tablespoons sake
1 tablespoon light soy sauce
1/2 teaspoon chili-garlic sauce (see page 250)

Mix all the ingredients together well in a bowl.

Ceviche Sauce

2 teaspoons aji amarillo (yellow or orange chili
*   paste, see page 250)*
1/2 cup fresh lemon juice
4 teaspoons yuzu juice (see page 253)
2 teaspoons soy sauce
1 teaspoon freshly ground black pepper
2 teaspoons finely chopped garlic
1 teaspoon finely chopped ginger
4 teaspoons salted water

Put all the ingredients into a bowl and mix
well until smooth and blended.

Mustard Miso

1 teaspoon Japanese or English powdered mustard
2 teaspoons hot water
5 ounces Den Miso (page 244)
2 tablespoons plus 1 teaspoon rice vinegar

1   In a small bowl, mix the mustard powder
with the hot water into a smooth paste, then
cover with plastic wrap and leave for an hour
to allow the mustard to develop its piquancy.

2   Mix in the rest of the ingredients to form
a smooth sauce.

Balsamic Teriyaki Sauce

1 cup plus 2 tablespoons balsamic vinegar
1 1/4 cups chicken stock
1/4 cup sugar
3 tablespoons plus 1 teaspoon soy sauce
3 tablespoons plus 1 teaspoon mirin
kuzu (see page 251), arrowroot, or cornstarch
*   mixed with a little water to thicken*

1   Put the balsamic vinegar into a
nonreactive saucepan and boil until it has
reduced by two-thirds.

2   Add the stock, sugar, soy sauce, and
mirin, and heat slowly until the sugar
dissolves. Bring quickly to a boil and whisk in
the kuzu to thicken.

3   Use while still hot. Any not used will keep
in the refrigerator for up to 3 days.

note   It is not necessary to use an expensive
balsamic vinegar, as the flavor is intensified
during the reduction.

Spicy Lemon and Garlic Sauce

7 ounces sake
2 tablespoons plus 2 teaspoons soy sauce
1 teaspoon chili-garlic sauce (see page 250)
1 heaped teaspoon finely chopped garlic
1/2 teaspoon finely chopped ginger
2 tablespoons plus 1 teaspoon fresh lemon juice
1 tablespoon yuzu juice (see page 253)
2 tablespoons grapeseed oil
2 tablespoons olive oil

1   Heat the sake in a saucepan to let some of the alcohol evaporate. Let cool to room temperature.

2   Mix this and all the other ingredients well together in a bowl. This will keep in the refrigerator for up to a week.

Yuzu Soy

5 tablespoons soy sauce
2 tablespoons yuzu juice (see page 253)

Combine the liquids together in a bowl and mix well. Store in the refrigerator for up to a week.

Sake Soy

2/3 cup sake
5 tablespoons soy sauce

Combine the liquids together and mix well.

Ponzu

1/4 cup soy sauce
1/2 cup rice vinegar
1/4 cup fresh lemon juice
about 3/4-inch square piece of konbu (see page 251)

1   Mix the ingredients together in a bowl and leave overnight to infuse.

2   Next day, remove the konbu before use.

Ama Zu Ponzu

3 tablespoons rice vinegar
5 tablespoons Ponzu (opposite)
2 tablespoons superfine sugar
1¹/2 teaspoons salt

In a saucepan over low heat, slowly heat the rice vinegar, Ponzu, sugar, and salt until the sugar dissolves. Remove from the heat and let cool.

Dashi

4¹/2 cups water
¹/3 ounce konbu (see page 251)
1 ounce dried bonito flakes (see page 250)

1   Heat the water and konbu together slowly in a saucepan over medium heat.

2   Just before the water boils, take out the konbu, add the bonito flakes, and turn off the heat.

3   Leave the stock until the bonito flakes sink to the bottom of the pan and then strain.

Dried Miso

3¹/2 ounces red miso (miso, see page 252)

1   With a metal spatula, spread the miso as thinly as possible on a silicone or nonstick baking sheet and place in a warm area to dry out naturally (24 to 48 hours).

2   Scrape the miso into a bowl and crush to a powder.

notes   The process can be speeded up by placing the sheet in a cool oven (225°F) for 1 to 2 hours, but take care the miso does not become too dark.
    Drying times may vary according to the time of the year.

Glossary

aji amarillo
This dried chili is orange, wrinkled, and tapers to a point. Its fruity flavor makes it suitable for chili sauces and stews. Aji amarillo paste is available as a commercial product in stores selling ingredients for South American cooking.

aji panca
This dried chili is dark brown, wrinkled, and tapers to a point. Its berry flavor and fruit tones make it suitable for chili sauces and fish dishes. Aji panca paste is available as a commercial product in stores selling ingredients for South American cooking.

aonori laver
Green seaweed; see Nori.

asari clams
Also known as the Manila or short-necked clam, these small clams are very popular in Japan for their tenderness and sweetness.

asatsuki chives
Similar to Chinese chives and green onions, asatsuki chives (*Allium ledebourianum*) can be shallow-fried as a vegetable or used as seasoning with sashimi.

ayu
This river fish (*Plecoglossus altivelis*) is caught with rod and line from June through August. Large specimens can be as long as 12 inches, but most are not even half that size. Ayu is usually eaten grilled or broiled with salt.

ayu tade
A peppery herb often used in the cooking of the ayu river fish. See Tade.

bamboo shoot skin
Known as *take-no-ko* in Japanese, the shoots of both the *Phyllostachys heterocycla* and *P. bambusoides* are a popular delicacy in Japan. The skin, which is usually peeled away before the shoots are boiled, can be used as an attractive garnish with strong hints of late spring, as are the plant's leaves.

bayberries
The purplish red fruit of the bayberry tree (*Myrica rubra*) is in season from late June to early July. The berries can be eaten raw, pickled in salt, or made into jam or a liqueur.

black cod
Also known as sablefish, black cod (*Anoplopoma fimbria*) is a dark-colored marine fish, which is caught in North American Pacific waters from the Bering Sea to Isla Cedros, Baja California. Black cod can reach a length of 36 inches and average 20 pounds in weight. Due to its rich oil content, it is exceptionally flavorful and an excellent fish for smoking. Despite its name, this fish is not in fact actually a member of the cod family.

black rice
Black rice is a glutinous and ancient variety of Japanese rice with a purple-black pigment in the rice bran. It has a concentrated flavor.

bonito flakes
Filleted bonito is steamed, dried, smoked, and cured with a mold (*Aspergillus glaucus*). When the fillets have become as hard as a piece of wood, they are shaved. This whole process takes many months. The flakes are used to make dashi and as a flavoring and garnish in numerous other dishes. In fact, dried bonito flakes are necessary in one way or another for making every Japanese meal. They are called *katsuobushi* in Japanese.

buckwheat
Called *soba* in Japanese, this herbaceous plant (*Fagopyrum esculentum*) is cultivated for its groats. The husk is removed and used as a filling for pillows. The groats are ground into the flour that is used to make soba noodles. Groats can also be cooked with rice or used for making beer or vodka.

chili-garlic sauce
This fiery sauce is made from a blend of fresh, roasted, or dried chilies and garlic, sugar, salt, vinegar, and other seasonings. It is called *tobanjan* in Japanese.

daikon
The giant white radish (*Raphanus sativus*) is an essential ingredient in the Japanese kitchen. Grated daikon is added to the tempura dipping sauce because it aids the digestion of oily foods. A green variety (*R. sativus var. longipinnatus*), often called green radiola or green mooli is also much used. Daikons are often cut lengthwise into a continuous sheet, using a special grater called a *katsuramuki*, for use in various preparations. The young shoots of the daikon, or daikon cress, are used in salads and as a garnish for sushi. See Kaiware.

dashi
Japanese stock is made from dried bonito flakes and konbu. Along with soy sauce, sake, and miso, it is one of the most important elements in Japanese cooking. (See pages 17 and 249.)

edamame
The Japanese term for fresh green soybeans.

enoki mushrooms
This winter mushroom (*Flammulina velutipes*) grows naturally worldwide, yet is known almost exclusively by its Japanese name. The sticky yellow-white cap is seldom wider than 1/2 inch, while the long, thin stalks are usually well over 5 inches. Enoki mushrooms are used in soups and stews, and broiled with chicken. Fresh enoki are exported from Japan in sealed plastic packages to keep them fresh.

eringi mushrooms (*pleurote du panicaut*)
Pleurotus eryngii is a wild mushroom with a dark brown cap to be found between June and October, growing to a height of between 3 and 8 inches. Its flesh is firm and fragrant.

flying fish roe
Also known as tobiko caviar, the tiny, bright orange, salted eggs of the flying fish have a mild, sweet, fishy flavor. Flying fish roe is used in small amounts as a tasty and decorative garnish for sushi and salads.

fruit tomatoes
Also known as sugar or perfect tomatoes, these small, sweet tomatoes can only be produced under special cultivation conditions that restrict the amount of water they are given. The yield is minimal, but their sugar content is as high as any fruit. Fruit tomatoes are not currently exported everywhere, but have been available in Japan for about 12 years.

gari
Thinly sliced ginger marinated in sweetened rice vinegar is served as a condiment in sushi restaurants so diners can refresh their taste buds between different types of sushi.

garlic shoots
These are the flowering stems of the garlic plant and look rather like a coarse chive stem. With a flavor like a cross between garlic and asparagus, they are available from Asian markets.

ginaan nuts
Better known by their Chinese name gingko, these buff-colored delicate, sweet nuts are popular in Japanese cooking.

gourd shavings
Known as *kanpyo*, strips or ribbons cut from the flesh of bottle gourds are sold dried. When rehydrated in lukewarm water, they are a popular sushi filling.

hajikami
These pickled shoots of the ginger plant are used to garnish many Japanese meals.

hamo
The complex meaty flavor of conger eel makes it a prized ingredient in Japanese cuisine. Filleting it is one of the great arts of the Japanese kitchen.

ice fish
The odd-looking, ghostly Antarctic ice fish is related to the much sought after Chilean sea bass or Patagonian toothfish and has some of its fine distinctive flavor.

ise lobster
This famed spiny lobster with a long beard and bent back is said to bring long life and wisdom. Festivals are held in honor of the delicacy.

ishigaki (giant) clams
The waters around the Japanese island of Ishigaki are famed for their giant clams.

ito-togarashi
Togarashi is Japanese for "peppers," and *ito* means "thread," thus ito-togarashi are long chilies cut lengthwise into long, fine threads for use as a garnish.

junsai
Sometimes called "water shield" in English, this tiny aquatic plant (*Brasenia schreberi*) has long, threadlike stems that grow up from the root. In early summer, the Japanese harvest the water shield's leafy shoots on the surface of ponds and pools. Junsai is sold loose in plastic bags or in bottles.

kaiware daikon
The young shoots of the daikon are used in salads and as a garnish for sushi. Cut off the root ends before using these sharp, spicy shoots.

kalamansi
This small fruit, also known as the sour lime, is small and round with slightly flattened ends. They can be picked green or ripe, but the juice stays sour. It is halved and placed alongside dishes of mixed fried noodles and similar one-dish meals, and squeezed over individual servings for a piquant flavor. The juice is used in a cordial concentrate, which is diluted to make a refreshing cold drink.

kanpyo
See Gourd shavings.

karashi su-miso
This is a miso mustard vinegar peparation that can be made at home or bought ready-made. You can use the Mustard Miso recipe on page 247.

katakuriko
The leaves and flowers of the dogtooth violet (*Erythronium japonicum*) are commonly used as a garnish in Japanese cooking. Flour made from the plant is much prized as a starch and is sometimes used as an expensive alternative to potato flour.

kinki
Known in English as the bighand thornyhead, this large red fish is a species of alfonsino (*Beryx decadactylus*) or bream.

kinoko mushrooms
Literally meaning "child of a tree," *kinoko* is the word for "mushroom" in Japanese, but the term tends to be used mostly as a generic for wild mushrooms.

kinome
Sansho sprigs are called *kinome* in Japanese. These young leaves are used as an edible garnish, chopped herb, or made into a paste. See Sansho.

kobe beef
Kobe beef is a special grade of beef from cattle raised in Kobe, Japan. The cattle are massaged with sake and fed a daily diet that includes large amounts of beer. This produces meat that is extraordinarily tender, finely marbled, and full flavored. It is also extremely expensive. Because of the high cost and increasing demand, there are now some Kobe-style beef-cattle being raised in the USA, Australia, and Scotland using the same techniques; this is often called waygu beef after the breed of cattle used.

kochujang
This is a thick, misolike fermented chili bean paste popular in Korean cuisine. Made from soybean paste, red pepper powder, and glutinous rice flour, it keeps almost indefinitely in the refrigerator. Some brands are hotter than others.

konbu
Konbu (*Laminaria japonica*) is a variety of kelp that grows in the cold seas off the coast of northern Japan, mostly around the northern part of Hokkaido. Rich in monosodium glutamate, konbu is sold in supermarkets as dashi konbu in fairly large pieces for use in making stock. This konbu should never be washed because the flavor lies on the surface. At most, wipe it clean with a cloth and don't leave it in boiling water. Konbu is also a well-known dietary source of iodine and rich in iron. *Shira ita*, or white konbu, is actually pale green kelp, which becomes almost translucent when marinated.

kuzu
Also seen as *kudzu*, this is an Asian vegetable, the roots of which are generally dried and ground into a powder that is used both as a thickener and as a coating for food being deep-fried.

lotus root
The underwater roots of the lotus water lily may be up to 1 1/4 yards long and are generally about 1 inch in diameter. Peeling their reddish-brown skin reveals creamy-white flesh with a crisp texture and a coconut-like flavor. The roots are available fresh, canned, dried, and candied.

madako octopus
The common octopus (*Octopus vulgarus*) reaches an average size of 24 to 36 inches in length. Called *madako* in Japanese, it can be found throughout the world's warm seas.

maitake mushrooms
This autumn mushroom (*Grifola fondosa*) is fragrant, tasty, and very versatile. It is best in a preparation called *maitake no kurumi*, in which the mushrooms are dressed with a walnut paste.

makomo-dake
Known in the West as water bamboo or Manchurian wild rice, this plant belongs to the same family as the common bamboo and is closely related to the wild rice of North America. The enlarged stems are harvested, the upper leaves cut off, and only the stems with husklike wrapper leaves sent to market. The edible portion is the succulent stem after the husks are removed.

mantis shrimp
Actually unrelated to shrimp, these crustaceans are referred to as shrimp because of their front appendages and how they use them to capture food. The description "mantis" is due to the fact they resemble the appearance and have the same hunting characteristics of a praying mantis insect. Mantis shrimp are popular in Japanese cuisine and often eaten as sushi.

masago
This is the roe of the smelt fish, which is often used as a sushi topping and garnish.

matsutake mushrooms
Of the many kinds of edible mushrooms that grow in Japan, matsutake mushrooms are said to be the king, because of their wonderful aroma and flavor. Matsutake grow in the red pine forests in the autumn, and are a special and very expensive delicacy in Japan at that time.

mirin
This liquid flavoring containing 14% alcohol is used in cooking for its sweetness, rather than its alcoholic content. Regular sake cannot be substituted for it.

miru (giant) clams
The Japanese term for the white surf clam. It has a mild, sweet flavor.

miso
This fermented paste of soybeans and either rice or barley with salt is an essential ingredient in the Japanese kitchen. It is combined with dashi in miso soup and also used as a flavoring for other foods. Red miso, Japan's most popular rice miso, is salty and rich in protein; white miso, on the other hand, is rather sweet. Made from fermented soybeans and barley, moromi miso is never used for making miso soup. This soft, dark brown paste is usually eaten with chilled cucumber.

mizuna
This feathery, delicate salad green (*Brassica campeatris*) is a mildly peppery pot herb that has been cultivated in Japan since antiquity.

molokheiya
This is Egyptian spinach or melokhai and has a bright green leaf with a soft texture when eaten. In both Middle Eastern and Asian cultures it is widely used in soups.

momiji-oroshi
This is a preparation consisting of grated daikon mixed with red-hot chili pepper. It can be bought already prepared or you can make it yourself quite easily by inserting seeds from a chili into a daikon on the tip of a chopstick and then grating the whole thing.

mongo cuttlefish
The common cuttlefish (*Sepia officinalis*) and the pharaoh cuttlefish (*S. pharaonis*) are both called *mongo ika* in Japanese. The former grows to a maximum length of about 10 inches and is familiar in the Mediterranean and east Atlantic. The latter is slightly larger and is prevalent from the Arabian Peninsula across to Japan and Australia.

mooli
See Daikon.

moromi miso
A type of miso made from fermented barley, but never used for making miso soup. This soft, dark brown paste is most often eaten with chilled cucumber.

myoga ginger
Because only the stems and buds of myoga ginger (*Zingiber mioga*) are eaten, it is hardly recognizable as a type of ginger. It isn't hot like regular ginger and its fragrance is more herbal. The buds are especially aromatic when thinly sliced and used as a garnish.

nigari
Nigari, or bittern, is a concentrated solution of various salts remaining after the crystallization of salt from seawater. The main ingredient should generally be magnesium chloride. Nigari is used as the natural solidifying agent in the preparation of tofu.

nikiri-zake
This sauce for sushi can be bought or made by mixing 1 part sake to 3 to 4 parts shoyu (Japanese soy sauce).

nori
Red laver—*asakusa nori*—is harvested and dried in paper-thin sheets of a standard size. The nori is then toasted and used for wrapping sushi rolls, rice balls, and futo-maki. Green laver—*aonori*—is harvested, dried, and sold in tiny flakes to sprinkle over food. *Aonori* is also an ingredient of shichimi togarashi.

pen shell clams
Also known as fan shell clam or mussel, this is a type of razor clam found embedded in the mud. Once highly popular in Japan, they are now becoming rare and highly prized.

ponzu
A citrus-and-soy-sauce dip (page 248).

red miso
Red miso (*akamiso*) is made from a fermented paste of soybeans and rice. It is red to brown in color and high in protein and salt.

red vinegar
This sweet and powerful rice vinegar made with sake lees that have been fermented with yeast and the koji mold for three years is the preferred choice of sushi chefs, because relatively little sugar is needed to make the shari-zu for vinegared sushi rice.

rice flour
Japanese rice is of the variety Japonica and is glutinous, or sticky. Ground to a flour, it is called *shiratamako* and is used to make sweet mochi dumplings.

rice vinegar
All vinegar produced in Japan is fermented from rice and is mild in flavor, with about 4.2% acidity. Non-rice vinegars cannot be used as substitutes.

rock shrimp
So-called because of their rock-hard shells, rock shrimp are valued for their lobsterlike texture and flavor.

rocoto chili paste
Also known as rocotillo, this relation of the habañero is orange-yellow or deep red when ripe, round with furrows, and tapers to a point. It is mildly fruity and has an intense heat. Essential for ceviches, rocoto chili paste is available as a commercial product in stores selling ingredients for South American cooking.

sansho
The seedpods of the Japanese pepper (*Zanthoxylum piperitum*) are ground and used as seasoning, especially as one of the seven spices in shichimi togarashi. The sansho is usually sold ground, as it keeps its fragrance quite well. Sansho sprigs (the young leaves are called *kinome* in Japanese) can be used as an edible garnish, chopped herb, or made into a paste.

shakkiri mushrooms
This wild mushroom (*Agrocybe cylindracea*) is found at the foot of willow and maple trees between spring and fall. It has a dark brown cap and grows to a height of between 4 and 6 inches. Its flesh is firm and crisp. Marketed as the shakkiri mushroom, nowadays it is cultivated and sold throughout the year.

shichimi togarashi
This "seven-spice mixture" is a snappy collection of seven dried and ground flavors: red-pepper flakes, roughly ground sansho, tiny flakes of mandarin orange peel, black hemp seeds, poppy seeds, tiny flakes of green nori, and white sesame seeds. It is available in three strengths—mild, medium, and hot—from Asian supermarkets.

shiitake mushrooms
The best-known Japanese mushroom (*Lentinus edodes*) is extensively cultivated and often available in its dried form. Its distinctive, pungent flavor goes well with Japanese food. Fresh shiitake are good as tempura, in stews, or simply grilled with a little salt.

shimeji mushrooms
This autumn mushroom (*Lycophyllum shimeji*) is known for its excellent flavor rather than its aroma. It has straw-colored caps about $1/2$ inch in diameter. Shimeji come in clumps that grow from a single stem, like miniature oyster mushrooms, at the base of pine trees. Cooking them releases a distinctive flavor and aroma, making them very suitable for soups and other simmered dishes, as well as mixed rice dishes.

shiso
There are both red and green shiso leaves. The red ones (*akajiso*) are mainly used to color umeboshi and other pickles. The green leaves (*aojiso*) have many uses as a herb, tempura, and garnish. Although it is called a perilla or beefsteak plant (*Perilla frutescens*) in English, shiso is actually a member of the mint family. Shiso buds are also used as a condiment, garnish, and, when very young, for tempura.

snow crab
This large crab (*Chionoecetes opilio*) is caught in the Sea of Japan in the winter months and served as sashimi, tempura, and in vinegared preparations. Snow crab meat is sweet and delicate, with a more fibrous texture than king crab. Its texture ranges from the tender longitudinal fibers of shoulder meat to the firmer fibers of claw meat.

soba
Buckwheat noodles can be eaten either hot or cold. In their simplest form, a dashi-based soup is poured over the boiled noodles for *kake-soba*. When eaten cold, the noodles are served on a bamboo strainer with a dipping sauce. This is called *zaru-soba* (*zaru* being the Japanese for bamboo strainer).

somen
These dried, fine wheat noodles are served cold with a chilled dipping sauce usually in the summer. The noodles are boiled very briefly and then immediately refreshed in cold water.

sudachi
This acidic citrus fruit (*Citrus sudachi*) is a smaller relative of yuzu. It is used in the summer and autumn while still green for its tangy juice and aromatic zest. Sudachi is rarely available outside Japan and lemons can be used as a substitute.

su-miso
White miso paste thinned with rice vinegar is often used as a dressing.

tade
This is the water pepper, smartweed, or knotweed plant (*Polygonum hydropiper*). The tiny leaves have a mild peppery flavor and are much used as a garnish for sashimi. The leaves and stems can also be cooked and eaten, and these and the seeds are often made into peppery condiments.

tatami-iwasi (dry-folded sardines)
Sold as sheets and looking a little like thin dried noodles, these are tiny baby sardines that have been quickly pressed and dried. They are used both as a crisp tasty snack and as a flavoring.

tatsoi
A type of white-stemmed bok choy, tatsoi is a very popular green vegetable in Japan. Its very regular and elegant rosette of leaves also make it highly decorative.

tiradito
Tiradito is a South American dish consisting of cut fish and ceviche seasonings. Its name is derived from *tirar* (Spanish for "throw") because the fish slices are thrown into the serving bowl.

tomyo pea sprouts
Chinese pea shoots (*dau miui* and *dou miao*) are the handpicked, tender leaves and stems of the snow or garden pea plants, and are used as a light seasoning or added to soups. In Japan, tomyo pea sprouts are cultivated hydroponically and produced throughout the year in bulk. Pea sprouts are more aromatic and delicately flavored than bean sprouts.

tonka beans
These are the seeds of the large tropical tonka tree (*Dipteryx odorata*). Their fragrance is reminiscent of newly mown hay and can be used as an adulterant to vanilla. They are said to lighten one's mood and be emotionally balancing.

tonkatsu sauce
Made from vegetables, fruits, and spices, this is Japan's version of Worcestershire sauce. Named after the Japanese word for pork cutlet, with which it is often served, its sweet flavor goes well with fried food.

toro
The belly of tuna is very pale in color and fatty. Highly prized for sushi and sashimi, it is considered the best cut of the fish.

udo
The white stems and leaves of this aromatic plant (*Aralia cordata*) are similar to asparagus in taste. The tender young stems can be eaten raw or boiled.

umeboshi
Sour and salty, these are often called Japanese salted plums, but are actually a type of apricot. They are much revered for their reputed health-giving properties.

wakame
This seaweed (*Undaria pinnitifida*) is used in miso soup, salads, and other dishes.

wasabi
Although similar in flavor, Japanese horseradish (*Wasabia japonica*) is less harsh and more fragrant than its Western cousin. Fresh wasabi is very expensive. It grows wild in cool, shallow pools of pure water, often high in the mountains, and is extensively cultivated under similar conditions. It can also be bought as a powder or paste from Asian supermarkets. *Wasabi zuke*, or pickled wasabi, uses the leaves, flowers, stems, and sliced rhizomes.

white miso
White miso (*shiromiso*) is made from a fermented paste of soybeans and rice or barley. It is beige to light brown in color and quite sweet. A high-grade Kyoto product, white miso is expensive.

yama-imo
This is a white root also known as mountain yam or mountain potato. It is cut into crisp slices as a crunchy accent to roe sushi, or grated and made into a cold porridge.

yama-momo
The Japanese term for the bayberry (*Myrica rubra*).

yariika squid
Yariika or spear squid (*Loligo bleekeri*) is a slender, spear-shaped cephalopod that grows to about 16 inches in length. Spear squid are caught in the seas around Japan, particularly in the spring when they come close to the coast to lay their eggs.

yuzu
Japanese citron (*Citrus junos*) is zestier than lemons and not as sweet. Yuzu also has a very potent fragrance. It is used for both its acidic juice and its aromatic peel. Yuzu juice is now available from Asian supermarkets.

yuzu kosho
Available from Japanese markets, this commercial seasoning comprises green chili, yuzu peel, and salt.

Index